DONCASTER
AND DISTRICT

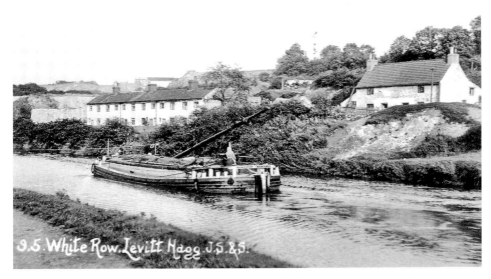

All the houses at Levitt Hagg were company property, and whenever an employee left or retired, the premises were vacated. Information gleaned from people who had relatives in Levitt Hagg during the Edwardian period reveals that nearly all the residents kept fowl or pigs. A 'Sick Club' was also formed, members contributing each month, and a payment of 10s per week 'sick pay' was granted for a limited period if absent from work.

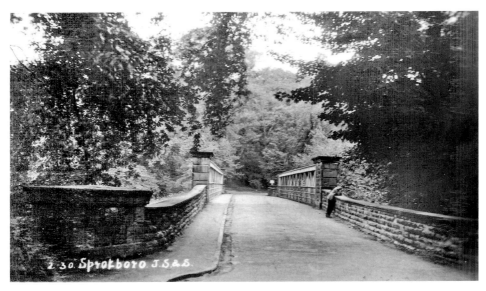

According to Kelly (1908), a beautiful bridge at Sprotbrough, in the Classic style, was built over the River Don at the sole expense of the late Sir Joseph William Copley, Baronet, and 'was presented by the late Lady Copley, about 1888, to the County Council, who have pulled it down and erected an iron girder bridge in its place'. The bridge underwent major repairs during 1978 when work totalling £40,000 was undertaken. During that time pedestrians were provided with a temporary footbridge.

DONCASTER AND DISTRICT

From the James Simonton Collection

PETER TUFFREY

AMBERLEY

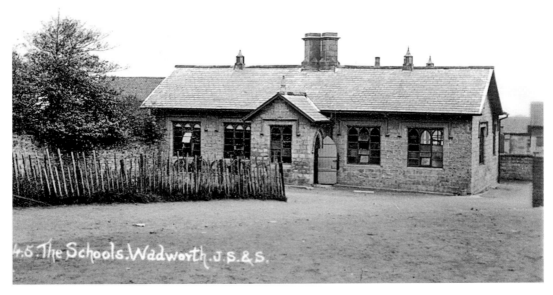

Wadworth Schools, which carry a date stone inscribed 1860.

First published 2012

Amberley Publishing
The Hill, Stroud
Gloucestershire, GL5 4EP

www.amberley-books.com

British Library Cataloguing in Publication Data.
A catalogue record for this book is available from the British Library.

ISBN 978 1 4456 0121 2

Typeset in 10pt on 12pt Sabon.
Typesetting and Origination by Amberley Publishing.
Printed in the UK.

CONTENTS

INTRODUCTION

I have a tremendous interest in old photographs and I tend to regard Victorian and Edwardian photographers as heroes. However, I feel that my adulation sometimes embarrasses their descendants. This was the case with Frank, Fred and Joan Simonton, relatives of the firm of James Simonton & Sons (J. S. & S.), which produced thousands of picture views of Doncaster and its environs between 1908 and 1950.

On meeting the three, I gave an appraisal of the company's work, highlighting the significant contribution it had made recording the town at the beginning of the radical twentieth-century changes. Of course they listened with interest, but in a way they were embarrassed.

This was because I appeared to know more about their ancestors' postcard work than they did; they had no J. S. & S. postcards themselves, and were unable to answer a proportion of the detailed questions I fired at them.

Joan and Frank were a little uneasy about confessing to me that they had little experience of ever using a camera. I tried to put all three at ease by stating that if they interrogated me for information about my grandparents, I would probably be equally as inadequate at providing any answers. Yet after much discussion and cross-referencing between the three relatives, I obtained about enough information on J. S. & S. to piece something together for this book.

James Simonton, grandfather of my three 'helpers' and founder of the J. S. & S. postcard business, came to Doncaster around 1908, settling in Wadworth. He was born in 1861 at Sandford, Dublin, where his father, also called James, had been partner in several photographic firms; and these were Edwards & Simonton, and Simonton & Millard. Later, however, he seemingly operated a prestigious photographic studio at 70 Grafton Street. A company letterhead in Fred's possession claims that this was established in 1854. It also states that James Sr was photographer to 'Queen Victoria' and the Lord Lieutenant of Ireland. There was also a studio in Jersey.

So, it is obvious that the J. S. & S. founder followed his father into the photographic trade. But, before embarking on the postcard view work, he became a photographer in the Royal Engineers, travelling to such exotic places as Ceylon and India. His wife, whom he met in Jersey, bore him three sons, James Jnr, Frederick and Francis.

'On leaving the army, my grandfather moved around a lot, as was customary for photographers in those days,' said Fred (Frederick's son), 'and eventually settled in Doncaster around 1908. Of course, at this time there was much happening in the town, and all three of his sons were initially involved with the J. S. & S. business.'

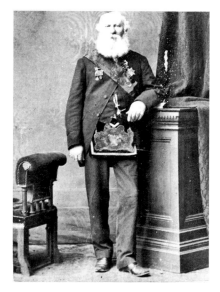 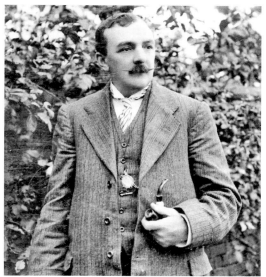

Above left: James Simonton Snr.

Above right: James Simonton, founder of the J. S. & S. postcard business.

'The family had a smallholding in Wadworth,' informed Frank (Francis's son), 'and my grandfather, besides being a photographer, also wrote articles for the *Allotment and Smallholder* publication.'

James Simonton settled in Doncaster during the period, which is currently recognised as the heyday of topographical postcard views of 1900–18. There were probably several reasons for their popularity:

1. Most postcards at this period cost a penny or less and could be posted with a halfpenny stamp in England.

2. Postcards were the best means of sending a message with a picture.

3. The postcard view allowed anyone to send a picture of their town village or street to a relative in any part of the country.

Several other postcard companies were operating in Doncaster besides J. S. & S. including the Roto Photo Co. Ltd, Regina Co. Press and Edgar Leonard Scrivens. Their work was in great demand.

J. S. & S. have produced literally thousands of topographical views and the range of subjects was enormous. Between 1908 and 1950 they photographed virtually every street and numerous local events, in towns and villages within a 20-mile radius of Doncaster. Their pictures have outstanding clarity, are beautifully composed and full of incidental details.

They not only photographed the former rural splendour of some of the villages, but recorded their evolution into sprawling mining communities.

The messages on the backs of the postcards illustrated here seem quite trivial today, and curiously do not bear any relation to the view depicted. Here is an example: 'Dear Ettie, Keep the gravy hot, hot, hot H.'

'They used to sell the views to post offices at 14s (70p) a gross,' informed Fred.

After initially operating from Wadworth, J. S. & S. moved to Warmsworth Road, Balby and then to Young Street in Doncaster town centre. James Jnr only participated in the business for a short time.

'He didn't see any future in it,' said Joan, 'and subsequently became a commercial traveller, continuing to do some photography in his spare time.'

The J. S. & S. founder died in 1931. Frank said he could recall very little about his grandfather, but Joan and Fred said that 'he had a fiery Irish temper'!

In the years following James Simonton's death, the postcard business and commercial photography itself were in the doldrums due to the depression. 'It was around that time,' stated Frank, 'I went canvassing for business with my father. We went from door to door, my father carrying his tripod and asking if anyone wanted their photograph taking.

'Sometimes when he delivered the photographs he had taken, people would say they hadn't any money to pay the bill. When I got back from my first taste of canvassing, I told my mother that the photographer's life wasn't for me and I was never involved again.'

Frank's father eventually left the business and worked elsewhere; he died in 1945. Frederick and his son soldiered on until finally calling it a day around 1959. From that time, the name of J. S. & S., synonymous with that of photography in Doncaster for more than fifty years, finally faded away. Disappointingly none of the company's glass plate negatives or archives survives today.

'The staggering prices of J. S. & S. postcards nowadays is what amazes me,' said Joan. 'Cards, which once sold for 1d and 2d, are now fetching between £10 and £60. If my father, grandfather and uncles were alive they would be totally confused and amazed.'

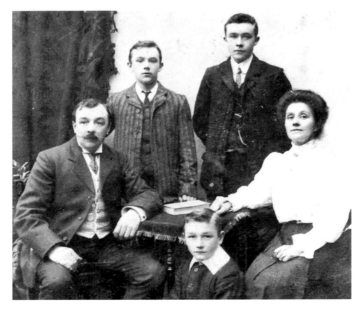

James Simonton, wife and three sons.

The growth of picture-postcard collecting over the last twenty-five years has been phenomenal. And it is probably the nostalgic appeal of the cards that makes them so collectable. They also reveal the vast changes that have occurred to the urban and suburban landscapes, especially in the Doncaster area. And we owe much to postcard-view photographers for capturing it all.

J. S. & S. never made much cash out of their work, but posthumous fame and regard is surely an adequate compensation.

Peter Tuffrey

ACKNOWLEDGEMENTS

I am grateful for the assistance received from the following people: Peter Davies (Doncaster Mayor), Ray Nortrop, Hugh Parkin, Derek Porter, the late Malcolm Stannage and Simonton family members.

Special thanks are due to my son Tristram Tuffrey for his help and support throughout the project.

BIBLIOGRAPHY

Abercrombie, P. and T. H. Johnson, *The Doncaster Regional Planning Scheme: Together with an Appendix on Coal Subsidence by Joseph Humble* (Liverpool and London: 1922).

Barrass, N., *Stainforth – Our Heritage* (Doncaster: 1986).

Hey, D. and J .R. Magilton, 'St Peter's Church Warmsworth', *Yorkshire Archaeological Journal* 55 (1983), pp. 27–59.

Hunter, J., *South Yorkshire: The History and Topography of the Deanery of Doncaster, in the Diocese and County of York* (London: 1828–31).

Kelly, *Kelly's Directory of the West Riding of Yorkshire* (London: 1908).

Magilton, J., *The Doncaster District: An Archaeological Survey* (Doncaster: 1977).

Morris, G., *The Story of Methodism in Doncaster and District 1743–1988* (Doncaster: 1988).

Pearson, F., *From a Quarry to a Park* (Doncaster: 1991). Peck. W., *A Topographical History of Bawtry and Thorne with Villages Adjacent* (1813).

Pevsner, N. and Enid Radcliffe, *Yorkshire: The West Riding (The Buildings of England)* (1958).

Platt. J., *Thorne's First Railway* (Doncaster: 1991).

Quick, M., *Railway Passenger Stations in Great Britain: A Chronology* (Oxford: 2009).

Seddon, P., *Loversall* (Doncaster: 1972).

Shaw, A., and F. Shaw, *Looking Back at Carcroft: A Photograph Album* (Doncaster Library Service, Doncaster: 1986).

Twistleton, J. F., *Moorends and Its Church* (1985).

W. E. A. Local History Group, *Sprotbrough in History Part 1* (Doncaster: The Workers' Educational Association Yorkshire District (South), 1968).

W. E. A. Local History Group, *Sprotbrough in History Part 2* (Doncaster: The Workers' Educational Association Yorkshire District (South), 1969).

1

ADWICK-LE-STREET TO BALBY

ADWICK-LE-STREET

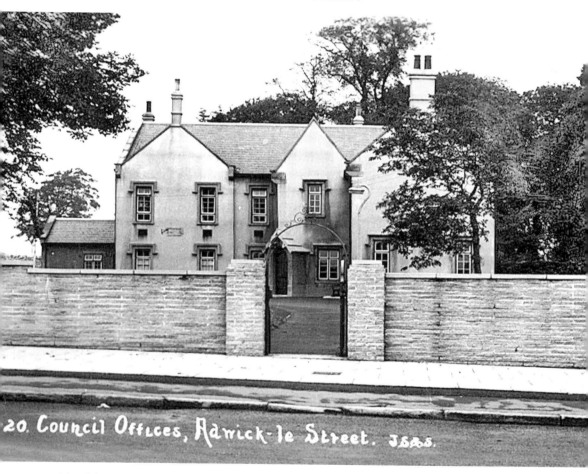

20. Council Offices, Adwick-le Street. JS&S.

Adwick-le-Street Urban District Council purchased Adwick-le-Street rectory in 1952 and an official opening occurred on 6 December 1955. A booklet, published to coincide with the building's opening, included the following information: '[the building] dates back to the reign of King Charles the Second, to be precise the year 1682 ... The Revd Joshua Brooke ... built at his own cost [in 1682] the present parsonage house from the foundation.' Adwick-le-Street Council's initial intention for the building was to house their treasurer's department.

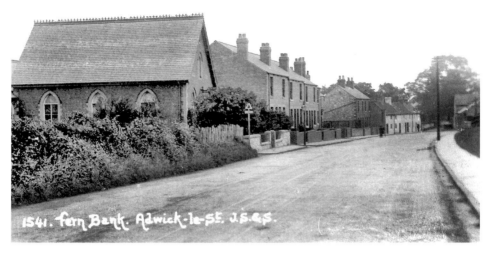

One of the most interesting aspects of Adwick-le-Street's history is its association with the Washington family and the first President of the United States. A branch of the family once lived at Adwick Hall, which is long gone. The church registers show that they were there from 1562 until two years after the birth, in Virginia, of the future president. They bought Adwick-le-Street in 1560 and their arms, stars and bars – from which the national flag of United States was derived – are sculptured on the family tomb. This view is taken from Redhouse Lane looking down Fern Bank to the junction of Mill Lane and Village Street. 'Fern Bank, 1910' is noted in a plaque on the properties in the centre, while all the properties beyond have been replaced by modern buildings. The Methodist chapel, partly obscured on the left, dates from 1887.

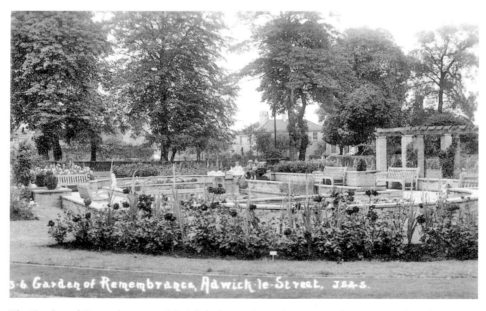

The Garden of Remembrance at Adwick-le-Street. According to Magilton (1977), the village name and present street pattern 'point to an especially interesting past; the name suggesting a Saxon origin to the settlement'. The original village of Adwick, centred on Village Street, was mentioned in the Domesday Book.

An unpublished and undated manuscript held in the Doncaster MBC Reference Library states that, following a search, no firm date for the construction of the mill could be found. And while the date stone on the house reads 1786, analysis of the land tax records for Adwick-le- Street reveals that the building was occupied in 1784. The mill was owned from 1784 until 1789 by Charles Duncombe and occupied by William Boulton. The Duncombe family at one time owned much land in the area and it has been suggested that they were responsible for the building of the mill and organised the engineering of the mill dyke. A newspaper advert dated 16 February 1842, for the sale of the mill, indicates that steam power had already been installed.

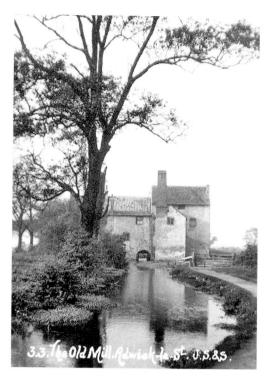

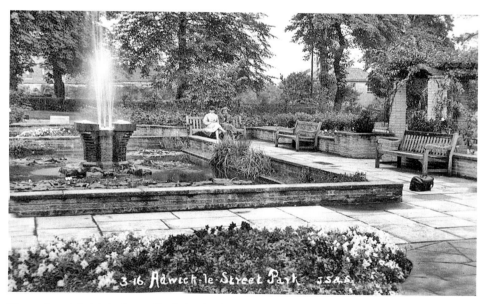

The park at Adwick-le-Street. Until the development of collieries at Brodsworth and Bullcroft (at Carcroft), Adwick had been the same quiet farming village for centuries but expanded in subsequent years. On www.doncaster.gov.uk it is stated that the Adwick-le-Street conservation area is based on the old settlement located around the church of St Lawrence. It is linear in character and stretches along Village Street with a spur along Church Lane; the latter was the main road to Carcroft before the village centre was bypassed by the building of Doncaster Lane.

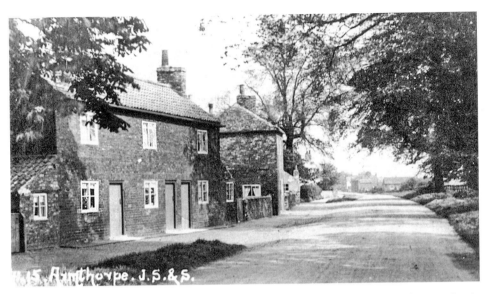

During the late 1920s Armthorpe changed from a quiet rural community into one that was deeply involved with coal mining. Earl Fitzwilliam was one of the landowners and he also owned the coal rights. Initial work at the colliery site had started around 1912. Victoria Cottages on Church Street, looking south, are depicted here. In 1922, Abercrombie and Johnson mention '[Armthorpe's] straggling village street of a mile in length is bound to develop as an offshoot of the colliery village, which lies at the opposite end nearer Doncaster.'

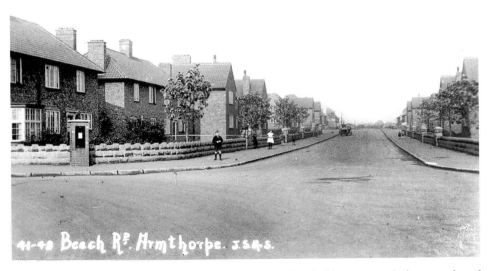

The *Doncaster Gazette* of 2 June 1922 reported that pit sinking had been resumed after a number of problems had been overcome, adding that 'with housing too a fair amount of progress has been made although it will be some time before the Markham garden village project can be realised'. Simonton has taken the picture looking down Beech Road from Briar Road.

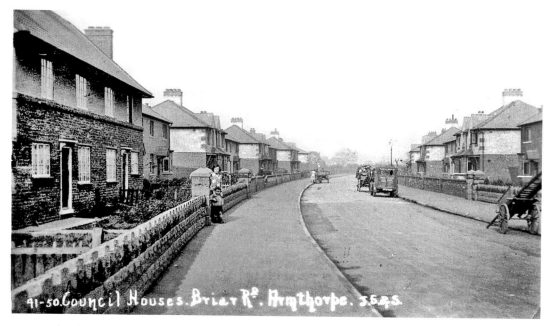

41-50. Council Houses. Briar Rd. Armthorpe. J.5&S.

Under the heading 'Colliery Housing Big South Yorkshire Scheme', the *Doncaster Gazette* (2 June 1922) stated that to meet the housing needs of the population in South Yorkshire, a company under the title of the Industrial Housing Association Ltd, with a capital of £1 million, had been formed by a number of leading coal magnates. No fewer than 10,000 houses were required in the South Yorkshire coalfield, and the bulk of these were required in the Doncaster district alone. 'Brodsworth, Bullcroft and Edlington require at least 300 and the Markham Main Colliery [at Armthorpe] will require a much larger number,' said the newspaper. From the air it can seen that the Armthorpe streets of houses are formed into rings or crescents. The top photograph shows Briar Road extending between Almond Avenue and Hawthorne Avenue; the one below illustrates Doncaster Road.

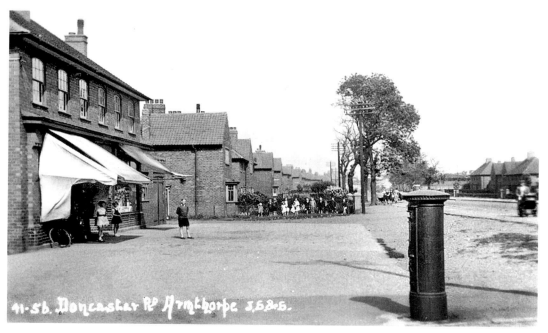

41-5b. Doncaster Rd Armthorpe J.5&S.

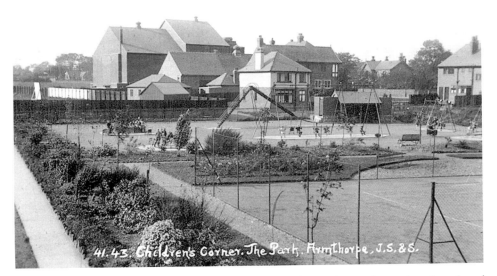

41.43. Children's Corner. The Park. Armthorpe. J.S.&S.

The *Doncaster Gazette*, 27 September 1929, said that with the opening on the previous Saturday of the handsomely laid-out recreation ground, provided under the Miners' Welfare Scheme, yet further facilities for social enjoyment were added to the fast developing colliery village at Armthorpe. The whole scheme, when fully completed, would cost £6,500. It was one of the very few schemes that made provision for golf, and a nine-hole course was being laid out. In addition the scheme made provision for an eighteen-hole putting green, children's playground and paddling pool, garden and shrubberies, bowling greens, tennis courts and a pavilion. The children's corner is illustrated above.

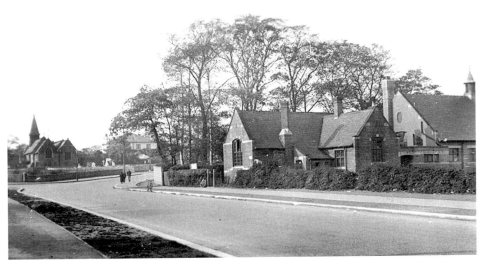

Here we see Church Street, looking towards the junction with Doncaster Road and Mere Lane. The St Leonard and St Mary church is on the left and the Parish Room on the right. The church is chiefly in the Perpendicular style consisting of chancel, nave, north chapel and an octagonal tower and spire. The register dates from 1653. The Parish Room was built on glebe land in 1887 and the total cost of the building was £450. With the population increase in the 1920s, an extension was planned and the foundation stone was laid by Miss Gertrude Bell on 6 September 1930. The architects were Allen-Hickson and the builders Pearson & Blackwell.

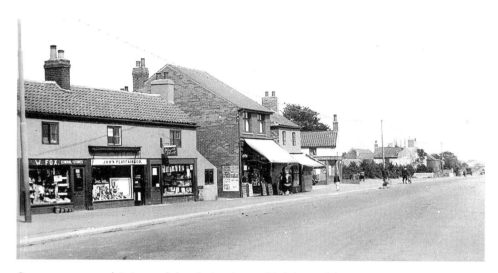

On www.num.org.uk it is stated that during the troubled times of the 1920s, entire mining regions suffered. Medical studies in the coalfields revealed that malnutrition affected a total of one million men, women and children in these communities. So terrible were conditions that a special Miners' National Distress Fund was set up. On 19 April 1929, the *Doncaster Gazette* mentioned that two new 'distressed areas', those of Armthorpe and Mexborough were authorised by the West Riding Divisional Committee of the Coalfields Distress Fund at a meeting in Leeds on the previous Tuesday. The business premises of W. Fox (general stores) and John Playfair & Co., may be identified here on Church Street.

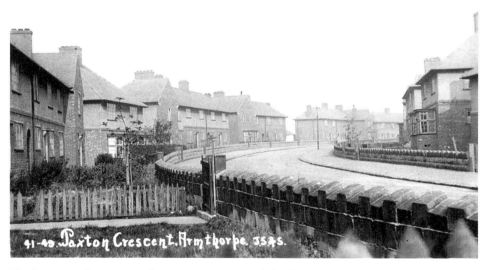

The *Doncaster Gazette*, 17 February 1922, mentioned that the uncertain situation in the coal trade, leading to the disastrous stoppage of the previous year, brought about a total cessation of the work at Armthorpe. Since that time many of the houses already completed in the Garden Village planned by Sir Tudor Walters had been occupied by miners working at Bullcroft and other parts of the district. Sir John Tudor Walters (1868–1933) was a British architect, surveyor and Liberal politician. He served as Paymaster General under David Lloyd George from 1919 to 1922 and once again briefly in 1931 under Ramsay MacDonald. Paxton Crescent, seen above, extends from Doncaster Road, cuts through George Street and Edward Street before completing a semi-circle to rejoin the first road.

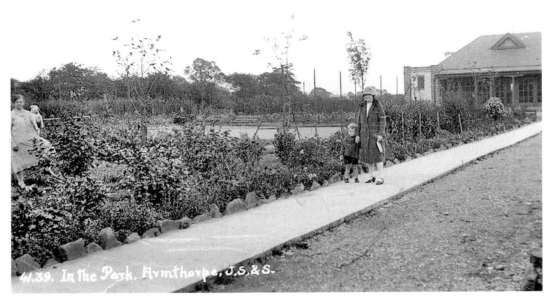

41.39. In the Park. Armthorpe, J.S.&S.

At the gates of the recreation ground on 21 September 1929, W. Humble, chairman of the Doncaster Collieries Association, formally declared the area open. A challenge shield was presented by the contractors for competition among the miners. Representative teams played bowls, tennis and golf, and selections were played by the Markham Main Ambulance Band. Speeches were also given by Ben Turner MP, Secretary for Mines, and Herbert Smith, President of the Miners' Federation of Great Britain. Smith said that although rapid strides had been made in providing recreation grounds and other schemes for miners there was still plenty to do. Since 1919, £8,428,253 had been spent in many ways – on recreation, health, education, research and pit welfare. Yorkshire had been very active and had administered £1,178,293. Tea was then provided in the Plough Hotel. The above photograph shows people posing for the camera in the park; the one below the paddling pool.

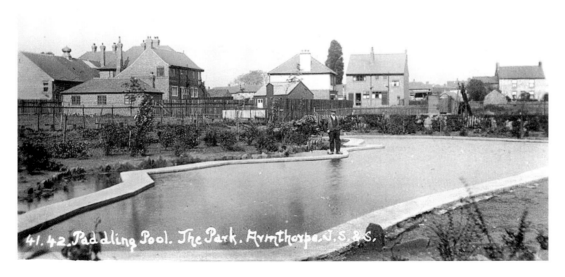

41.42. Paddling Pool. The Park. Armthorpe J.S.&S.

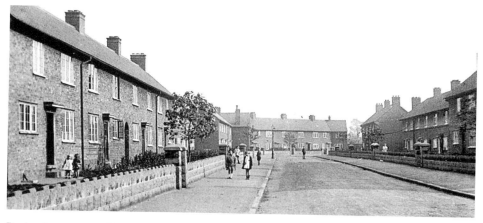

During August 1929, Doncaster Rural District Council applied to the Ministry of Health for sanction to borrow £19,995 to carry out the Armthorpe sewerage and sewage disposal scheme. At a meeting held between the two bodies, some interesting facts were revealed. The area of Armthorpe was 2,023 acres. The population in 1911 was 381; in 1921, 625; and in 1929 about 5,500. At the meeting it was stated that the village's existing draining and sewerage was totally inadequate. Dr Duane, the Medical Officer of Health, said that they had been singularly blessed by providence in that they had escaped serious illness in the village through the present method of sewage disposal. Pictured is Poplar Place, a crescent, extending from Beech Road.

ASKERN

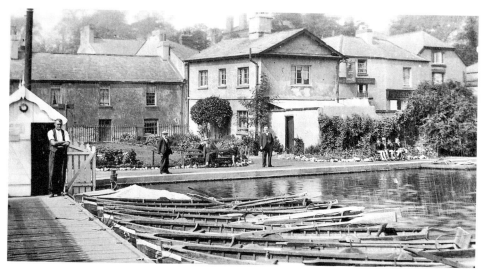

Askern was a spa – the general term used to describe a place at which mineral water baths were taken. During the late eighteenth century and early Victorian days, the fashion for taking holidays at spas and taking the waters increased. Askern remained a small, popular spa town until the early twentieth century. The sinking of the colliery changed its character and details are included in the *Doncaster Gazette*, 20 September 1912: 'The site chosen for sinking came as a shock to the Askern villagers, for instead of being somewhere on the levels between Askern and Moss, the head works were set up by the picturesque road to Campsall, right on the border of the spa itself, and within a stone's throw of the hydro and the famous pool'. A group of boats on the Askern lake are seen here along with the caretaker's cottage in the centre.

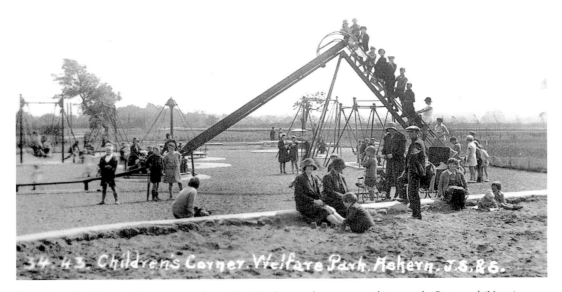

54·43 Children's Corner Welfare Park Askern, J.S.&S.

The Askern Coal & Iron Company was formed in March 1910, by agreement between the Bestwood (Notts) and Blaina (Monmouthshire) companies, to work the coal under the Campsall and Campsmount estates close by. The first sod was cut on 22 February 1911. None of the customs from the spa era survived after the colliery was sunk. The picture probably dates from the 1930s, shortly after the Miners' Welfare Park was opened in May 1930 by colliery owner Sir Samuel Instone.

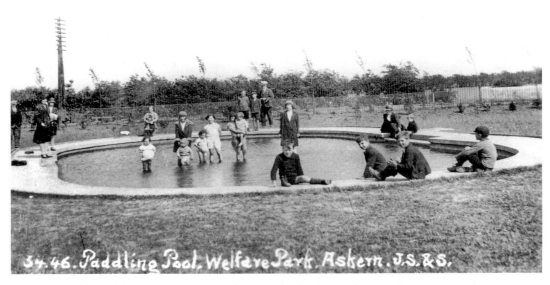

34.46. Paddling Pool. Welfare Park Askern. J.S.&S.

This picture of the paddling pool in Welfare Park was probably taken at the same time as the one above, as the card numbers are close to each other. With the introduction of the Mines Act (1930) and the quota system, Askern colliery operated at only approximately 66 per cent of its capacity and this continued throughout the decade. The result was that approximately 700 Askern miners were made redundant.

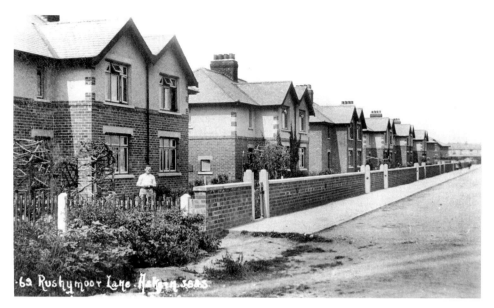

The *Doncaster Gazette* (20 September 1912) stated that the transformation of the old-world Askern village was proceeding apace. Rushymoor Lane, extending from Moss Road, is pictured here. A model village located between the colliery and Sutton Road was built for miners by the Askern Coal & Iron Co. under the company Askern Estates Co. Ltd from 1911. Goldthorpe builder Leadley won the contract to build a projected 2,366 houses at a density of thirty per acre. In time, workers came from a number of areas in the country to find work at Askern, including the West Midlands, Northumberland, Wales and Scotland.

BALBY

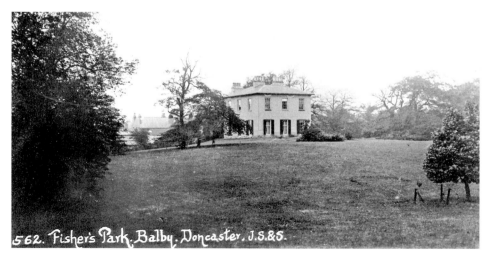

Westfield House, situated in Fisher Park, off Balby Road was for many years the home of Frederick Fisher, Doncaster's town clerk between 1824 and 1835, and also his son F. W. Fisher. The house was built during the early nineteenth century and in 1913 a 'suffragist' outrage occurred there, with two people being charged. By 1937, the house and grounds were acquired by Doncaster Corporation. In subsequent years the house was demolished and the grounds utilized as a park.

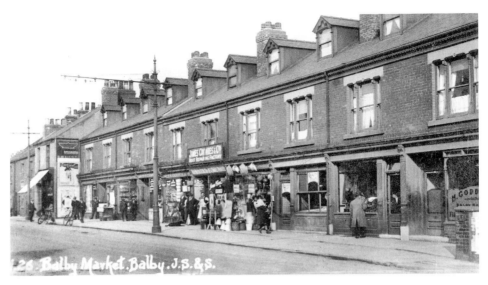

Balby Road was formerly part of the Tinsley & Doncaster Turnpike Trust, and the main western route out of the town. Also, it was once much longer than it is today. The 1852 OS map shows the thoroughfare stretching from the middle of Balby to the St Sepulchre Gate/Cleveland Street junction. The present Balby Road extends from Balby Bridge to St John's Road. The 'Balby Market' on the south side of Balby Road, and to the east of the junction with Carr Hill, is depicted here. Noted amongst the traders is James Coombe & Co.'s Boot Repairing Factory.

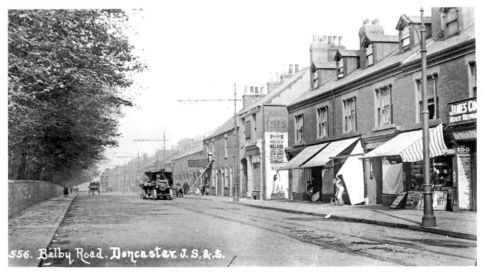

Balby Road has been photographed looking east towards Doncaster town centre. On the left are trees in Westfield Park. Balby Road carried the Balby tram service, which commenced in 1902, and from the Shakespeare's Head, the route was single track with passing loops at the Balby Steam Laundry, Carr View, Burton Avenue and Balby church. When the route was extended to Warmsworth in 1915 further loops were added. Baines (1822) recorded only sixteen residents in Balby itself. These included several gentlemen, a curate, two licensed victuallers (presumably at the Shakespeare's Head and White Swan), a miller, skinner and wheelwright.

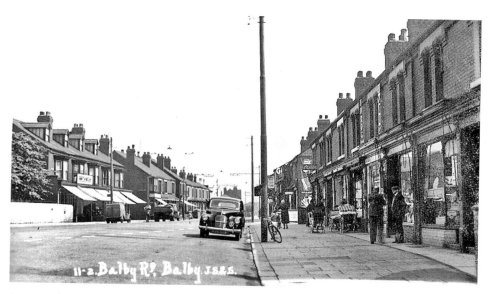

Simonton has captured High Road, Balby, from Low Road, looking east towards Doncaster. All the properties on the right have since been demolished for the 1960s dual carriageway construction, which has truncated Low Road, making it no longer accessible from this point. The demolished properties included the Oak Garage Co.'s premises. It is clear from the Plans Register, in the Doncaster MBC Archives Department, that much of the building work took place along High Road during the latter half of the nineteenth century. Also, it is tempting to suggest that the flurry of building activity during this period was linked to the coming of the railways, as Balby, along with Hexthorpe, became the town's first railway suburbs.

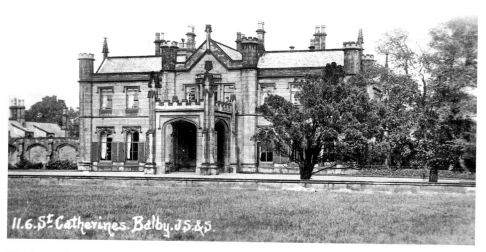

Hunslet wool merchant George Banks erected St Catherine's Hall around 1827. He died there in 1845 and his beneficiary was daughter Georgiana, who married the vicar of Loversall. By 1854 the vicar had adopted the name of Banks and when he and his family left the hall in 1866 it was leased to a number of tenants. The vicar's son, George James Banks (born in 1850), subsequently returned there and following his death in 1901 members of his family occupied the hall. Later it was purchased by a consortium of Doncaster businessmen who intended to develop the area, but was acquired in 1932 by the local Health Authority. St Catherine's has remained with the Health Department since that time.

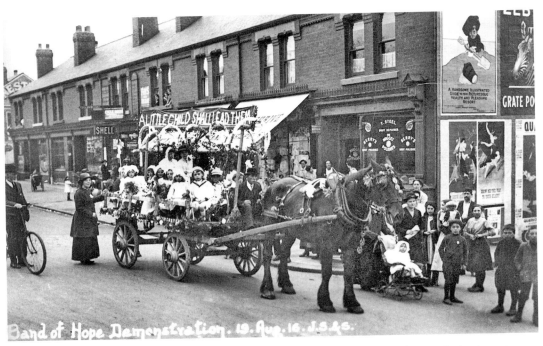

A Band of Hope demonstration moving along Low Road, at the junction with Grange Avenue, during August 1916.

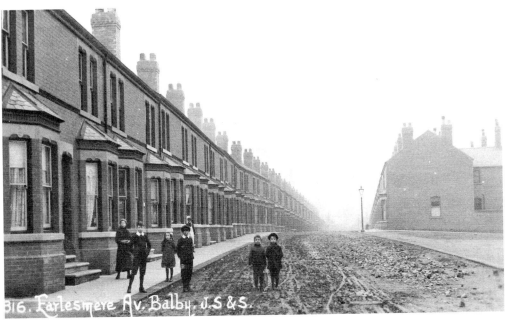

Earlesmere Avenue, extending between Balby Road and Florence Avenue. There are deposited plans in the Doncaster MBC Archives Department that include 'Earlsmere Avenue, Balby, plans of New Streets, July 1911', 'Earlsmere Avenue, Estate Plans, Aug 1915' and 'Earlsmere Avenue, 12 Houses May 1914'. The photograph shows the thoroughfare looking north.

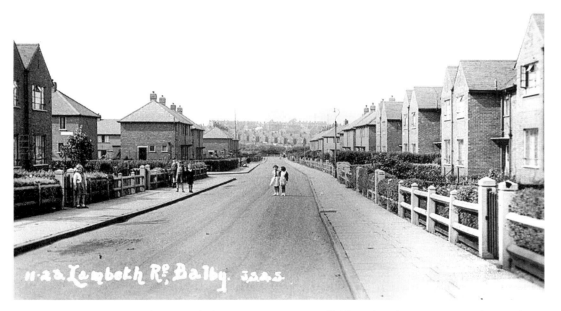

Lambeth Road is seen facing north, from a viewpoint in Woodfield Road, with Sussex Street and Surrey Street to the left.

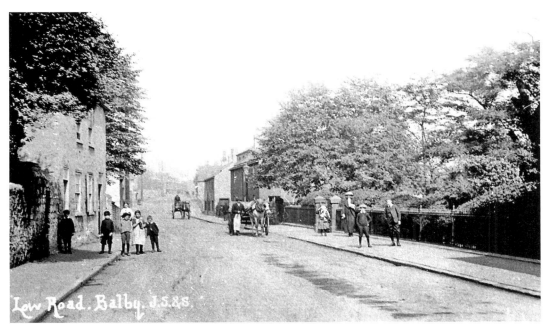

Simonton has taken this picture of Low Road, looking north-east, towards High Road, Balby. As previously mentioned, this road was truncated in the 1960s with the construction of the dual carriageway in High Road. The picture probably dates from around 1920, and at that time the Low Road business premises included those belonging to the Boot & Shoe beer house; J. W. Temple, coal merchant; and H. Jinks, coal merchant. Nothing is recognisable in this area today.

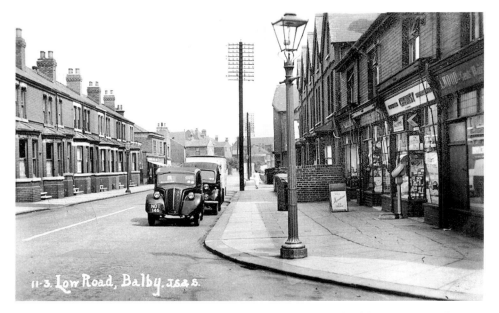

Low Road is seen, facing east, from the junction with Oliver Road. Much of the property is still extant, except the road does not link at the far end with High Road. Luxury apartments have also been constructed in recent years in the distance on the north side of Low Road. The business premises on the right include those once belonging to: H. Gittings, butcher; K. M. Lee, central stores; L. Edwards, chemist (note weighing scales in front of shop); and A. Wood, hairdresser.

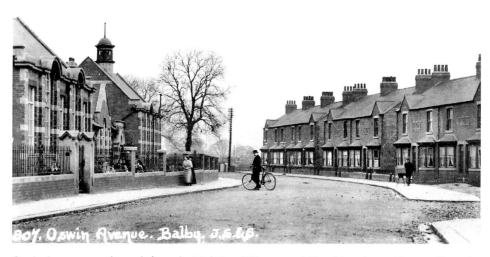

Oswin Avenue extends north from the High Road/Warmsworth Road junction to Harvest Close. On the left is Oswin Avenue school, and plans were received for the building in 1911. The plans were drawn by J. Stuart, architect to the West Riding Education Department. The school provided accommodation for 700 children. Plans for the Oswin Avenue estate were deposited in 1915.

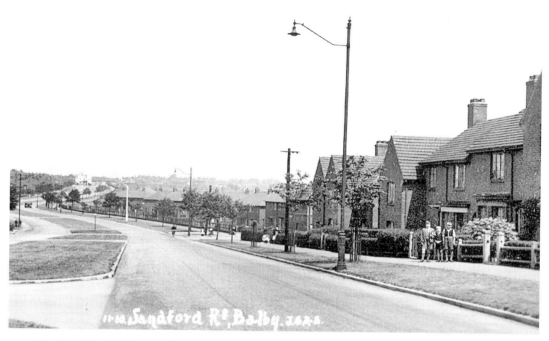

Sandford Road, facing north-east with High Road in the distance; the frontage of the White Swan public house is quite distinctive in the distance.

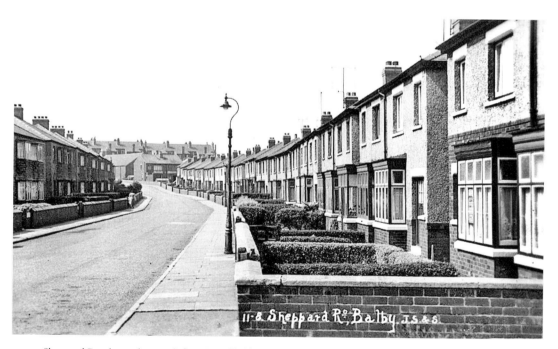

Sheppard Road stretches north from Woodfield Road to Low Road. Plans were submitted during December 1932 for 31 Sheppard Road, houses 1 to 61. Plans were submitted during December 1932 for 31 Sheppard Road houses, Nos 1–61. In May 1933 plans were deposited for twenty-five houses, Nos 2–50.

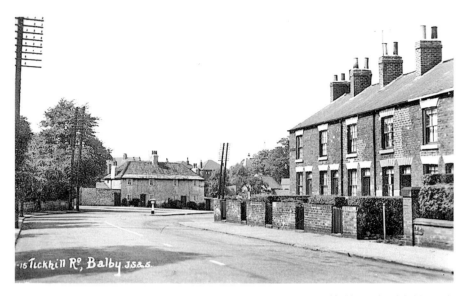

Tickhill Road has been photographed facing the junction with Woodfield Road/Ashfield Road/ Cross Street. Kelly (1908) mentions that Balby and Hexthorpe are pleasant villages, forming a parish, governed by an Urban District Council formed 1 April 1896, under the provisions of the 'Local Government Act 1894'. At one time the Balby Council offices were a short distance from here. The Doncaster MBC Plans Register notes housebuilding along Tickhill Road in small numbers from the late nineteenth century until the mid-twentieth century. The row of properties on the right has since been demolished.

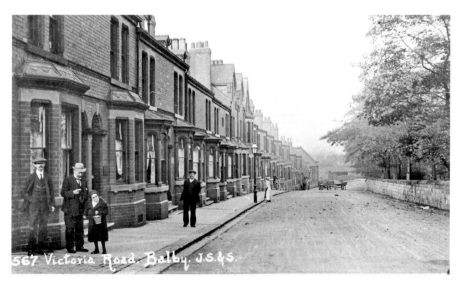

Victoria Road extends north from Balby Road to Florence Avenue. On the right are trees in Westfield Park and in the distance, on the left, the King Edward Road/Victoria Road School. The majority of house building along Victoria Road took place in small batches during the first half of the twentieth century. Plans were submitted for the school in 1907 and 1908. The view is another example of Simonton, recording changes in the local scene as they were unfolding. The area on the right was built upon later.

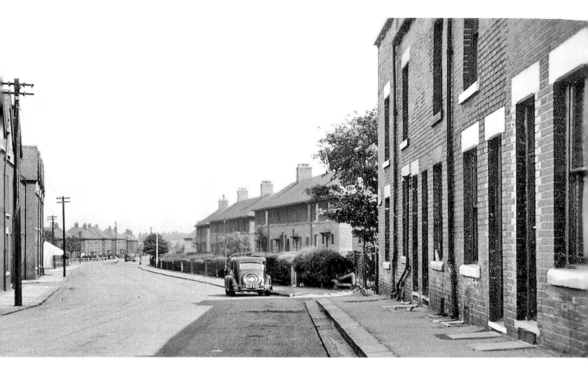

Two views of the 'northern' stretch of Woodfield Road. In the top picture Simonton has pointed his camera towards Sandford Road, and in the one below to the junction with Tickhill Road.

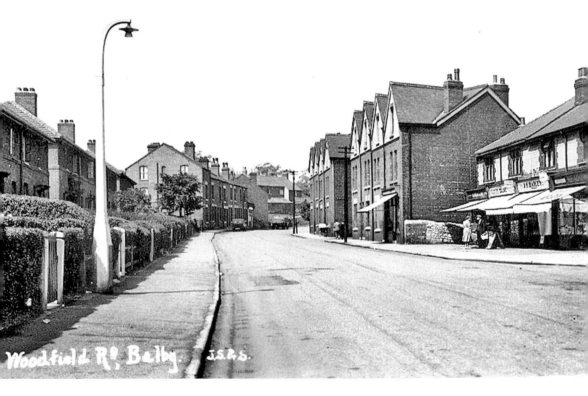

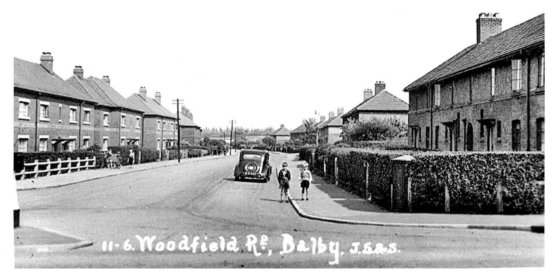

11-6. Woodfield R?, Dalby. J.S.&S.

Here we see the 'southern' section of Woodfield Road; the photograph was taken from the Sandford Road junction.

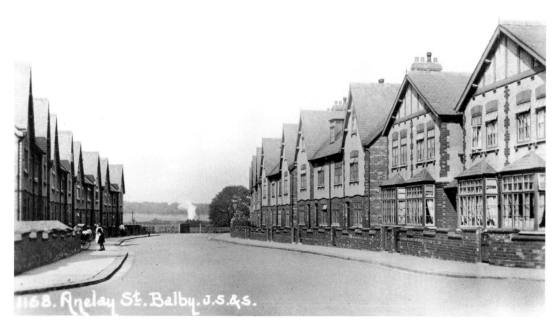

1168. Anelay St. Balby. J.S.&S.

This thoroughfare is presently known as Anelay Road, not Anelay Street as the title reads. Simonton has taken the view looking north towards St Peter's Road. Smoke from a steam locomotive working on the Sheffield–Doncaster line is just visible.

2

BARNBY DUN TO CARCROFT

BARNBY DUN

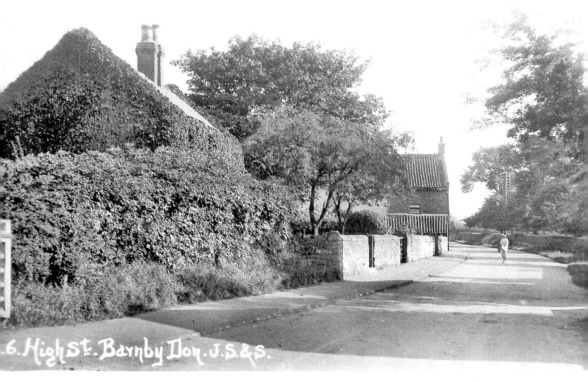

6. High St. Barnby Don. J.S.&S.

Barnby Dun is situated near the River Don and is 5 miles north-east of Doncaster. It is one of the few villages in the Doncaster area that has been unaffected by mining developments. At one time the village had its own railway station, two public houses, Wesleyan and Primitive Methodist chapels, and a public primary school. One noted private resident was George Milnthorpe, who had a malt kiln in the area. In 1921 Barnby Dun was linked with Kirk Sandall and Edenthorpe to form a civil parish. Edenthorpe was not included from 1956. Much demolition and infilling has taken place on High Street since the picture was taken, making it virtually unrecognisable from the view here. Barnby Dun was home to the Thorpe Marsh power station before its closure in the mid-1990s.

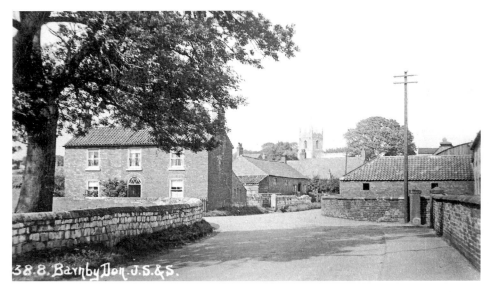

This is a view of the Madam Lane/Church Lane junction with the church of St Peter and St Paul in the distance. The church is a stone building in the Gothic style and the register dates from 1599. To the left, the area has been redeveloped and is occupied by housing.

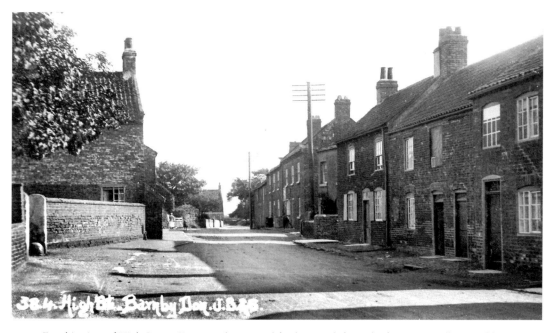

For this view of High Street, Simonton has moved further north from the first picture illustrated here of the thoroughfare. The principal landowners at Barnby Dun during the early twentieth century were George Milnthorp, the trustees of the late Mr Ross, the trustees of the late William Hunt, and Lord Allerton. Kelly (1908) notes the following amongst the commercial residents: butchers, farmers, bricklayers, a threshing machine owner, wheelwright, blacksmith, cowkeeper; most could be found for many years along High Street. The population at this time was approximately 600.

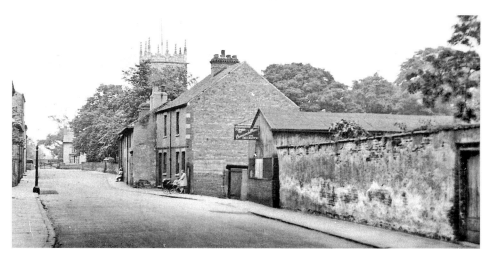

In the past, Bawtry was described as a well-built market town, on the Great North Road and on the line of the Great Northern Railway. Church Street, extending between Gainsborough Road and Wharf Street, runs parallel with the Great North Road and is south of the latter thoroughfare. Simonton is standing in Church Street and looking east to the junction with Wharf Street. The church of St Nicholas, partially rebuilt in 1696 and restored in 1833, is in the distance. David Hey (1986) gives earlier details of Bawtry and the church: 'A new town was laid out during the late twelfth or early thirteenth century, and by the second quarter of the thirteenth century Bawtry was a borough with regular markets and fairs. The church of St Nicholas stands beyond the grid pattern of the town … and was probably the focal point of the earlier settlement.'

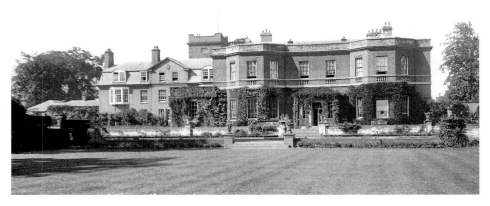

Joseph Hunter (1828–31) states that the present Bawtry Hall was constructed following the sale in 1779 of Bawtry Manor to Pemberton Milnes. William Peck (1813) adds, 'The old part of a family mansion was taken down [presumably by Pemberton Milnes] and the present structure erected on the site.' After Milne's death in 1795 the property was occupied by his daughter who married twice and died in 1835. The last private owner of the Hall was Major Peake, who acquired the property in 1904. Around 1905 he added a wing to the Hall and vacated the property at the outbreak of the Second World War. Bawtry Hall was occupied from 1939 by the West Kent Regiment until 1941, when it was taken over by the RAF and used by them as the headquarters of No. 1 (Bomber) Group. During the 1980s, the hall was vacated by the RAF and subsequently occupied by the Christians Reaching the World organisation.

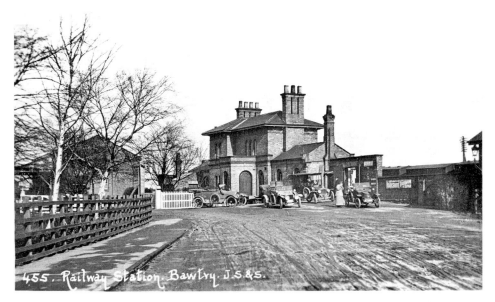

455. Railway Station. Bawtry. J.S.&S.

Bawtry railway station was opened by the Great Northern Railway Company on 4 September 1849. It was situated between Retford and Rossington on the East Coast Main Line and the main buildings were on the down side of the line. Closure came on 6 October 1958 but Quick (2009) notes an excursion from there to Bridlington on 3 April 1961. On 30 April 1971, goods facilities were withdrawn. The station was also used by royalty attending Doncaster races. The site has been cleared, but a couple of goods yard buildings have been converted for housing.

BENTLEY

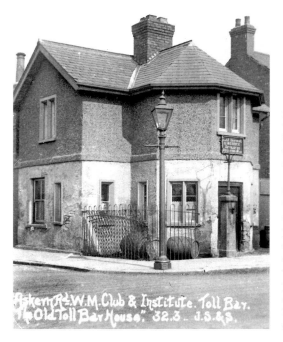

Askern Rd. W.M. Club & Institute. Toll Bar. "Old Toll Bar House". 32.3. J.S.&S.

At the turn of the nineteenth century, Bentley and Arksey's population was nearly 2,500, but this was to change considerably after the first sod was cut for Barber & Walker's colliery in March 1905. The figure given for 1910 was an estimated 7,500. By November 1911, the Bentleywith- Arksey ratepayers had decided at a meeting to apply for urban powers in order to govern their own affairs. At that time they were under the control of the Doncaster District Council, who it was claimed did not give them a proper return for their money. As a means of catering for miners' needs, the Askern Road Working Men's Club & Institute was established in the Old Toll Bar House.

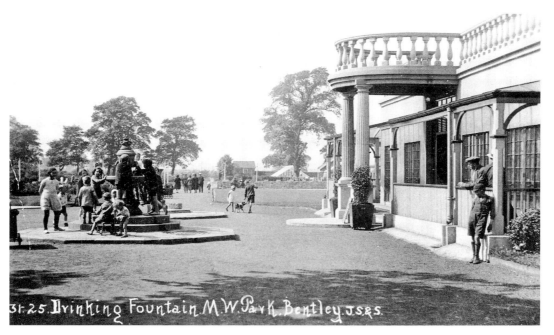

31.25. Drinking Fountain M.W. Park. Bentley. J.S.&S.

During 1923, a joint venture between the Miners' Welfare Scheme and Bentley Urban District Council led to the opening of public recreation area on approximately 18 acres of land near Askern Road and Cooke Street on Saturday 15 September of that year. Presiding at the opening ceremony were the chairman of Bentley UDC and a Minister for Mines. The recreation ground's facilities included bowling greens, tennis courts, pleasure grounds, a sand pit and play area. Obviously on his visit to the area, Simonton found plenty of interest to produce this view of the Drinking Fountain.

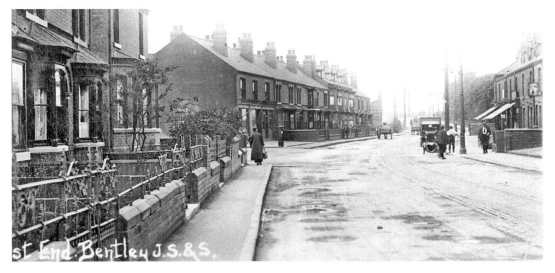

st End. Bentley J.S.&S.

Simonton is standing near the Bentley Road/Cusworth Road junction and pointing his camera northeast towards the bridge over the Doncaster–Leeds railway line. Bentley Road formed part of the Bentley tramway route; trams operated to and from Bentley between 1902 and 1928. Thereafter the route was served by trolleybuses until the early 1960s.

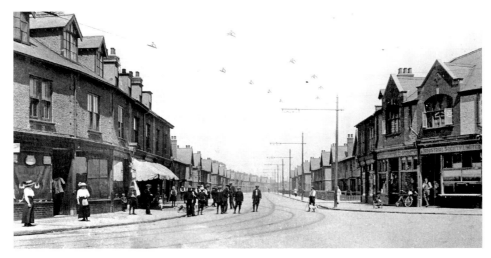

Simonton's camera is pointed in a north-easterly direction along the Avenue from a standpoint in Arksey Lane. The tram route was extended from the original terminus in Bentley High Street, and along the Avenue to a short distance from the colliery on 20 March 1913; the pit obviously having boosted passenger traffic on the route. Colliery owners Messrs Barber Walker & Co. produced plans for 802 houses at New Bentley, or Bentley New Village, as they called it in 1908. The Avenue, nearly a mile long, cut through a grid system of housing. The plans were drawn by local architect Philip Brundell and included twenty-four villas for pit officials, two large detached houses for the manager and agent, and 776 miners' cottages. The bricks for the houses were supplied by Barber & Walker's Watnall brickworks in Nottinghamshire.

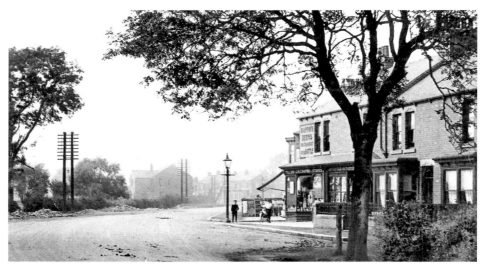

During August 1914 the housing situation in Bentley was becoming desperate. From a private census taken by a surveyor, it appeared there were 250 families living in lodgings, waiting for houses – the result of which was overcrowding. At the same time, a public enquiry was held into the application of the Bentley-with-Arksey UDC for sanction to borrow £26,017. This was for the purpose of a scheme, under Part III of the Housing of the Working Classes Act 1890, for the purchase of land and the erection of working-class dwellings. It was submitted that the population had risen by 100 per cent over the previous three years and stood then at about 12,500. Perhaps significantly, there was no opposition to the scheme at the enquiry. In the above view Simonton has photographed developments taking place along Owston Road.

BRAITHWELL

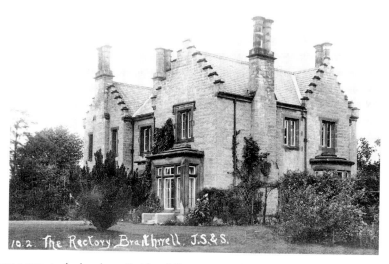

10.2. The Rectory Braithwell, J.S.&S.

According to a recent sales brochure, Braithwell Rectory, in Holywell Lane, dates from 1840. Its use as a rectory ceased in the early 1950s. The brochure also adds that the stone-built house originally had at least three live-in servants, and the servants' quarters were very different in character from the grander and larger rooms used by the original rectors' families. In 1991 a major project was undertaken to build a detached triple-garage in the style of a coach house, with a large garden store. At the same time the kitchen was extended and a large utility room built. A conservatory has also been added to one of the bays at the front.

BRODSWORTH

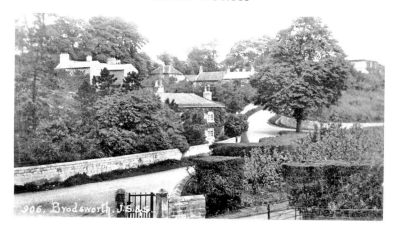

906. Brodsworth. J.S.&S.

Simonton is standing on the north side of the B6422 and pointing his camera at a small crossroads, which surprisingly still has much the same appearance today. Behind the trees is Brodsworth Hall, the former home, for over 120 years, of the Thelluson family and latterly the Grant-Daltons. Much of the property seen here would have belonged to the Brodsworth Estate. Brodsworth was designated a conservation area on 19 November 1990 and within this there are nineteen listed structures, including the Grade I listed Brodsworth Hall and Grade II* listed church of St Michael. Brodsworth Hall is now open to the public and belongs to English Heritage, who made the bold decision to conserve the interiors 'as found', rather than replacing or restoring them.

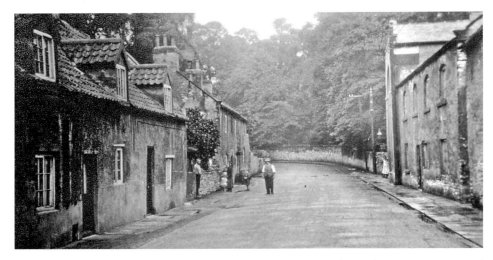

For many years Campsall's principal landowners were the Cooke-Yarboroughs at Campsmount and the Bacon Franks at Campsall Hall. But this had changed by the 1950s. The Cooke- Yarboroughs left the area, and Campsmount was demolished around 1945, while Campsall Hall was converted to flats during the early 1950s and demolished in the mid-1980s. Simonton is standing in the middle of High Street facing east. Beyond the trees was Campsall Hall. On the right is the Old Bells public house, which can be traced back to at least 1814.

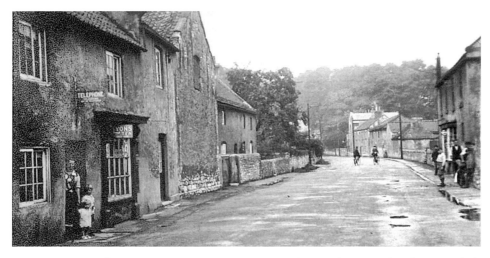

Moving westwards from an earlier position, Simonton has taken another view of High Street, which forms the backbone of the Campsall conservation area, designated on 21 December 1970. On www. doncaster.gov.uk it is stated, '[In Campsall] Limestone was the traditional material, which is rendered on some buildings. Principal roof materials are slate and clay pantiles. Limestone boundary walls are an important and extensive feature of the conservation area. The conservation area has numerous mature trees particularly within the site of the two old estates. Within the conservation area there are 19 listed structures.' Several buildings on the list are located in High Street and include Rose Cottage, Grade II, Manor House, Grade II and the Old Bells public house, Grade II.

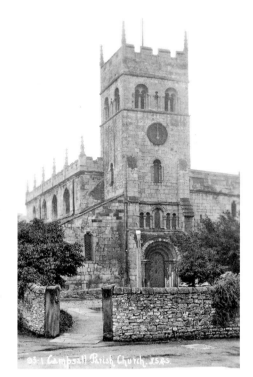

Kelly (1908) noted that the church of St Mary Magdalene, originally Norman, is a cruciform building of stone, consisting of chancel, nave, transepts, aisles, south porch, and a tower containing a clock, provided in 1879. He also adds that 'traces of the Norman church still remain, particularly in the tower, which is entered by a beautiful Norman arch; the chancel is Early English, and the nave perpendicular, but retaining portions of earlier work'. The church was restored in 1874, under the direction of Sir George Gilbert Scott RA at a cost of £4,000. The register dates from 1563.

CARCROFT

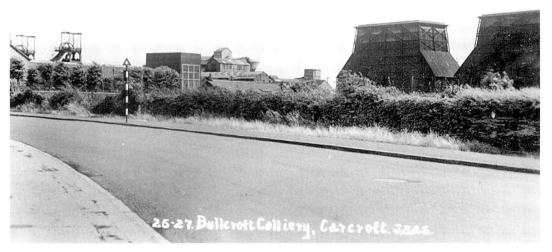

Coal was reached at Bullcroft colliery, Carcroft, in December 1911. It was the Barnsley seam, 9 feet thick and beneath the estates of several noted landowners. Sinking had commenced in 1908 and problems with water had to be overcome before success was achieved. By 1913 Bullcroft's workforce numbered approximately 1,800 and men had been drawn from Derbyshire and Nottinghamshire. The colliery closed during September 1970 and 700 of the workforce were transferred to Brodsworth a short distance away. Forty men were made redundant.

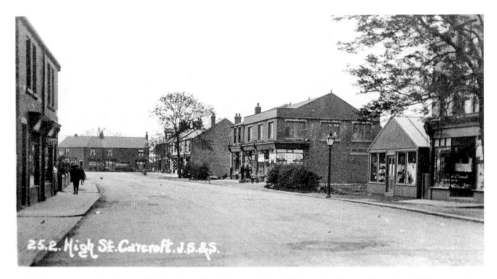

High Street stretches from Skellow Road to Owston Road (formerly Corpse Lane) and Simonton has taken the photograph facing east. Prior to the sinking of Bullcroft colliery, the thoroughfare consisted of mainly stone properties on one side, and trees and fields on the other. On the right various commercial premises are under development, with trees and bushes still part of the scene. The 'Provident Stores' are off to the right and were built in 1913. They were better known as 'The Thrift'. The building on the extreme right was occupied by Ford's pawnbrokers, Culley's, milliners, Akham's, ironmongers and was demolished for the Asda supermarket extension.

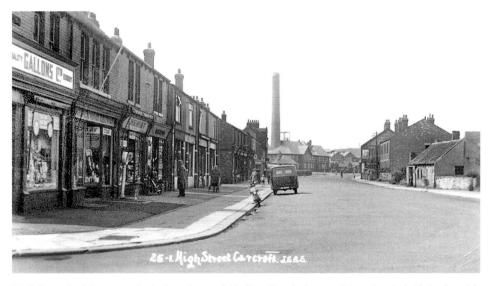

High Street looking towards the junction with Skellow Road; the new Moon Inn (rebuilt in the mid-1920s on a different site) and a chimney at Bullcroft colliery are also visible. Built from around 1913, the commercial premises to the left include those belonging to Gallons Ltd (previously Turner's). The last remnants of the old stone properties along the thoroughfare may be identified on the right. The building depicted formerly housed a forge. Shops further along were built by a Mr 'Turp' Ogden and have been occupied by a number of traders including Harrison's greengrocers, Thompsons' butchers and, presently, a chemist's pharmacy store.

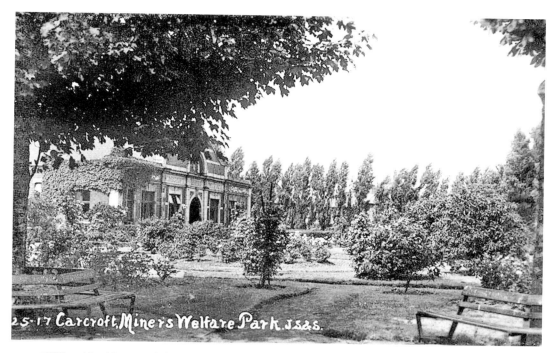

William Humble opened the Carcroft Miners' Welfare building, Welfare Park and Recreation Building on Saturday 31 January 1925. The area covered 10 acres of land and was acquired for £1,000 from local land owner Mrs Davis Cooke. A grant was obtained by the Bullcroft Miners' Welfare from the British Miners' Welfare Fund.

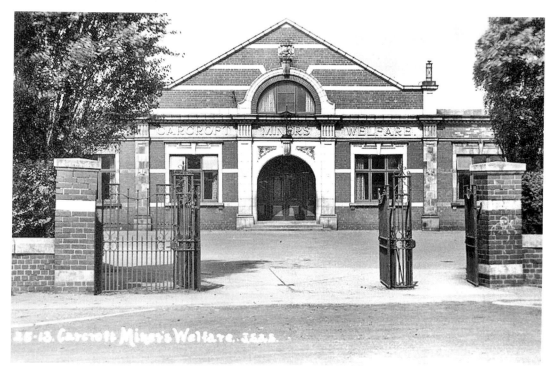

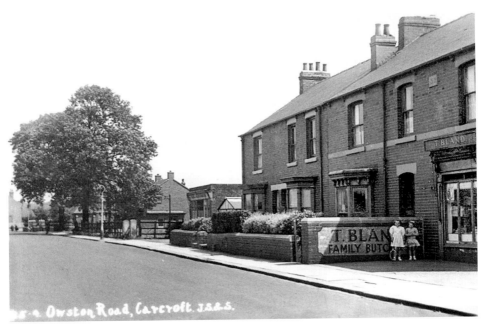

View from Gallon's Corner looking up Park Lane (now Owston Road), which stretches to the junction with Lodge Road and Owston Lane. Radiating from Owston Road are Paxton Avenue and Markham Avenue, which were part of the Carcoft New Village when the colliery was first sunk. Andrew and Frank Shaw (1986) state Park Lane was once called 'Corpse Lane' as a reminder that funerals once passed that way. They also add that 'there was little change or growth [in Carcroft] for perhaps 400 years until coal was discovered; farm workers turned to the pit for a living and the village grew to accommodate the new workforce. With this discovery, many of the traditions of the old farming community were destroyed.'

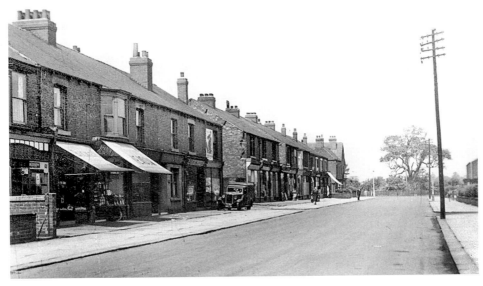

Simonton is positioned on Owston Road looking north to the junction with High Street. The stretch of commercial properties on the left, probably dating from around 1913, still survives today and fulfils the same purpose.

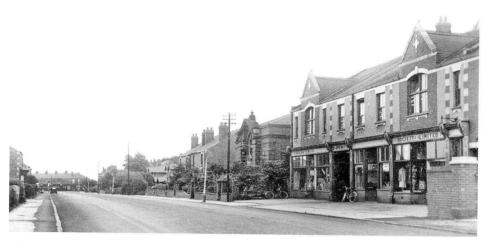

The view is looking east along Skellow Road to the junction with Station Road and Owston Road. On the right is the Co-operative Society building and a Methodist Chapel. The *Doncaster Chronicle* of 16 May 1913 praised the new Carcroft housing: 'In many respects most of the houses at Carcroft, Owston and Skellow set an example to colliers' homes in other parts even of the Doncaster district. They are larger and roomy, almost every house has its bath, its hot and cold water, and its w.c. The streets for the most part [as can be seen here] are wide and spacious, and in contrast to the grimy and monotonous villages on the other side of Doncaster, the place around Bullcroft makes a little paradise.'

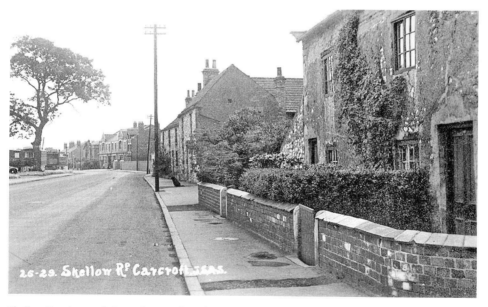

Skellow Road extends from Cross Hill to the Station Road/Askern Road junction. Simonton has taken this photograph looking east towards the junction with High Street. To the left of the telegraph pole is the Co-operative building. Cottages off-centre to the left were later demolished to facilitate a lay by for buses. Frank and Andrew Shaw (1986) mention that one of the properties in the foreground was formerly occupied by a Mr and Mrs Seal. They also add that 'on the left can be seen fairground caravans; Harniess's, Tuby's and Doubtfire's fairs visited the village 3 or 4 times a year'.

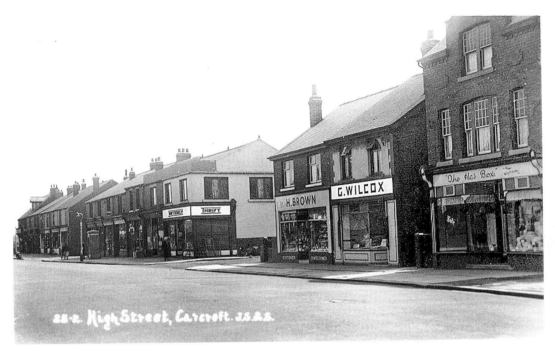

High Street looking south-east; the business premises include those belonging to the Thrift Stores; H. Brown; G. Wilcox; and The Hat Box. The latter premises were demolished for an extension to the Asda stores. It is interesting to compare this picture with one of a similar view on an earlier page.

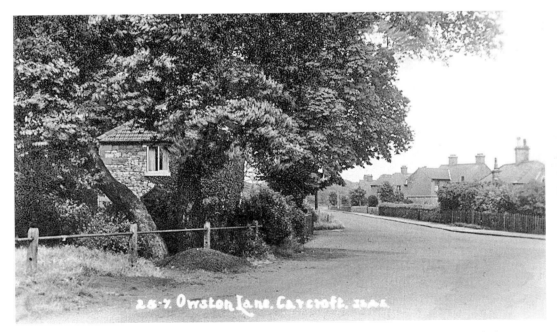

Simonton has captured Owston Lane facing east with Carcoft Lodge on the left. Andrew and Frank Shaw (1986) state that until around 1890 the Lodge had a thatched roof.

3

CONISBROUGH TO HICKLETON

CONISBROUGH

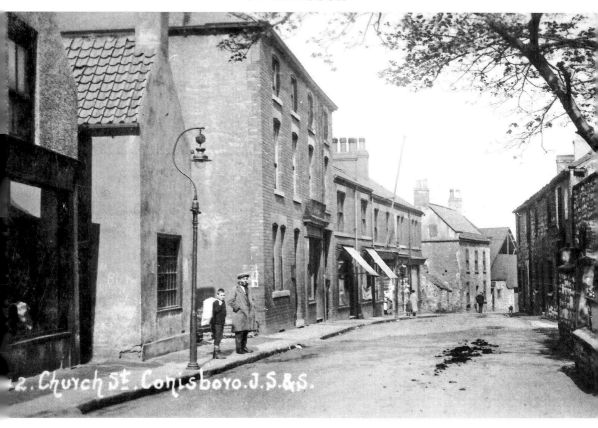

2. Church St. Conisboro. J.S.&S.

Church Street, facing north, is pictured shortly before the advent of Mexborough & Swinton trolleybuses, operating between the late 1920s and early 1960s to and from Conisbrough High (Conanby). Some of the buildings in the centre belong to Church Farm and existed until the early 1960s. Many of the buildings on the right were removed when the road was widened around 1950. This work also involved alterations being made to the church boundary wall and the construction of a flight of steps leading to the churchyard. Conisbrough Castle and church are out of view to the right.

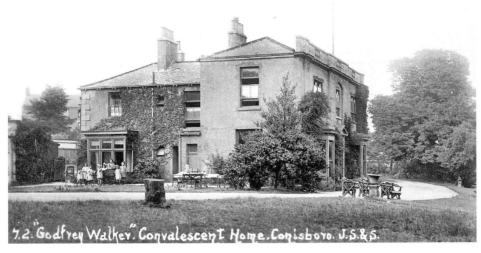

The Priory or Godfrey Walker's convalescence home, as it became known for a time during the twentieth century, is still extant and situated on High Street, Conisbrough. Godfrey Walker was senior partner in a local brick works, Walker & Crawshaw, and after his death, his widow gave the house to the Sheffield General Infirmary as a convalescence home for children. Judging from the number of children in the picture, Simonton clearly took the picture around the time the house was used for that purpose. The home was closed in December 1937, and during the Second World War the building was used for civil defence purposes. In recent years the building has been used as offices by the Doncaster Metropolitan Borough Council.

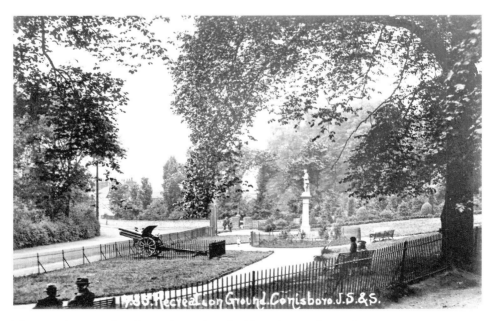

The recreation ground or Coronation Park at Conisbrough opened on 22 June 1911 to commemorate the coronation of George V. On the day of the event a lamp and fountain was unveiled on the park's periphery. The items were made by George Wright of Rotherham at a cost of £30. Mrs Godfrey Walker, travelling from her home in Scarborough, officiated at the ceremony. She had donated the land for the park and about £150 to cover other expenses, including the laying of footpaths and fixing iron railings.

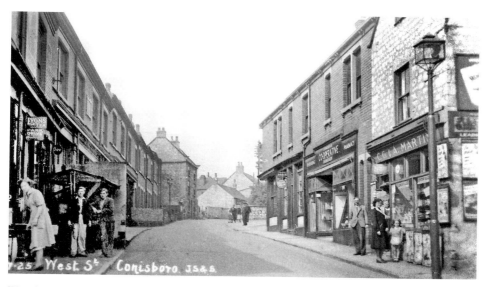

West Street stretches between the Beech Hill/New Hill junction and Church Street. The view is looking north-west to Church Street and on the left is the Doncaster Mutual Co-operative & Industrial Society Ltd's premises which carry a date stone of 1889 (visible in the top left of the photograph). Other business properties identified on the right include those belonging to C. O. & A. Martin and the Doncaster Co-operative's Chemist and Pharmacy store. Simonton has obviously caught the attention of locals and shopkeepers judging by the number posing proudly and eager to be included in the picture.

DENABY

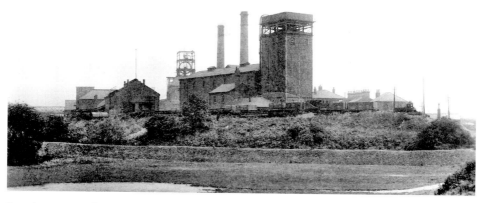

Denaby Main Colliery was opened in the 1860s by owners John Buskingham Pope and George Pearson. The colliery was well positioned for the transportation of coal, being adjacent to both the River Don and the Sheffield & Lincolnshire Railway. In the post-war years at Denaby there were 1,450 men working underground and 400 on the pit top. During 1958 Denaby and Cadeby collieries were linked underground and ten years later Denaby closed. Some men were made redundant but others transferred to Cadeby. Nothing now remains of the old Denaby pit site. Simonton has probably taken this photograph from Pastures Road looking east.

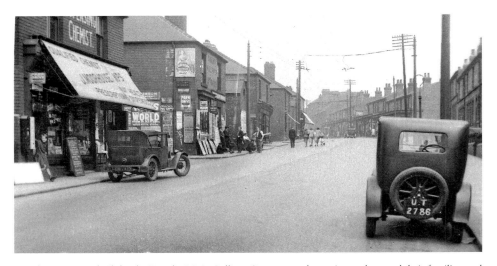

Denaby Main was built by the Denaby Main Colliery Company to house its workers and their families, and originally given the name Denaby Main Colliery Village, to distinguish it from the village of Denaby. From that time, the old village became known as Old Denaby. The view is looking east and the Denaby Main Hotel, in the distance, is the only survivor of the scene today. Yet, the premises are functional as an Indian restaurant, not a public house. During the 1970s, areas of late-nineteenth-century colliery housing were cleared and new properties constructed by the Doncaster MBC. The area depicted once contained many of the shops frequented by locals and included the business premises of J. Moorhouse and David Haigh.

DONCASTER

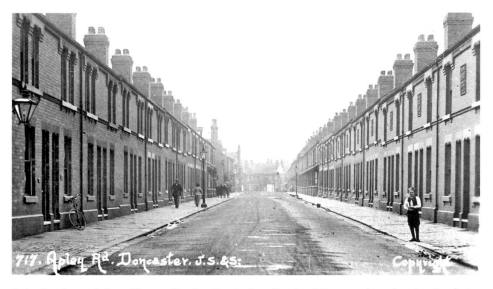

Apley Road extends from Chequer Road to Cunningham Road and Simonton has taken the view facing west. The Planning Register in the Doncaster MBC Archives Department notes there were a number of plans submitted for housing in Apley Road between 1890 and 1893. The houses were mostly erected by speculative builders and included the names of Gregory, Moate Duckett Co., Stevenson, Crawley, and Lamb & Patrick. The houses were probably built to meet the demand due to the influx of workers from other parts of the country as Doncaster grew in importance as a manufacturing base for the Great Northern Railway.

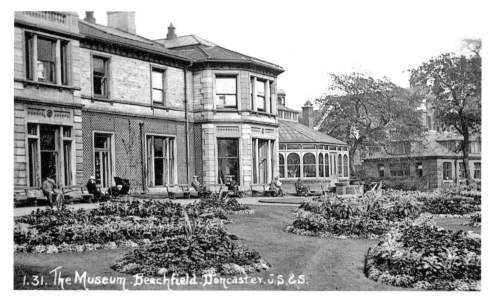

Beechfield House was built around 1812 by Henry Preston on a close or pasture ground, called Chequer or Waterdale Close. The house stood in almost 5 acres, containing ornamental planting, a meadow and kitchen gardens. By 1829, Beechfield was owned by the Revd William Cuthbert, who ran a private school on the premises. His occupation lasted another nine years until J. W. Sturgess, owner of the Bowling Ironworks, West Yorkshire, acquired the property. Two years after his death in 1861, his widow sold Beechfield to William Henry Foreman, who extended and altered the house and also improved the gardens. He then leased the property to several tenants including G. Morris and Richard Morris. The latter eventually transformed the grounds at Beechfield, featuring fountains, caverns and lawns and frequently opened them to the public. Morris's wife continued to live at Beechfield seven years after his death in 1900, when the Trustees of W. H. Foreman estate offered the house and adjoining lands to Doncaster Corporation for £12,500, which was accepted. Doncaster Corporation opened an art gallery in Beechfield House on 28 October 1909 and Viscountess Halifax officiated at the ceremony. The remainder of the building, after conversion for museum purposes, opened to the public on 23 March 1910.

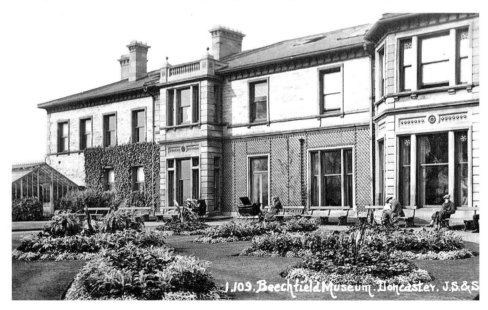

49

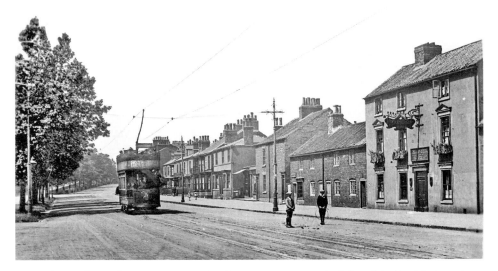

Bennetthorpe, facing the town centre with a Racecourse tram on the left and the Rockingham Arms public house on the right. From the Mansion House in the town centre to the Racecourse, the tram route was double-tracked. Trams operated on the Racecourse route between 1902 and 1930. Thereafter it was operated by trolleybuses. The original Rockingham Arms was erected in 1778 and the first host was William Bennett, from whose family the name of Bennetthorpe was derived. The Rockingham was rebuilt in the English Renaissance style during 1926. It was designed by local architects, Allen & Hickson.

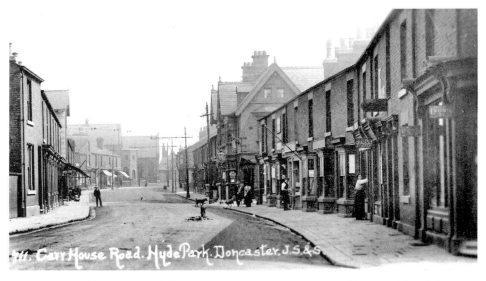

Carr House Road facing east, with the entrance to Catherine Street just visible on the left and the Prince of Wales public house in the centre. Only the buildings in the distance survive today, the remainder being demolished in the early 1970s for the construction of the Southern Relief Road. An 1852 OS map shows Carr House Lane – a bridle road – extending from Green Dyke Lane to the Racecourse. A short spur on Carr House Lane's south-eastern side once led to Carr House and its estate, after which the route is presumably named. House-building at Carr House Road, largely to cater for the influx of railway workers, appears to have begun shortly after the 1852 OS map was surveyed. References to the Hyde Park Tavern and Prince of Wales beer houses, situated along the route, date from the mid-1850s.

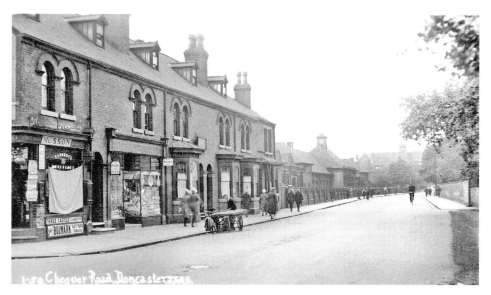

Chequer Road extends between Carr House Road and Waterdale. Simonton has taken the photograph facing north with Beechfield Road out of view to the left. House-building largely took place on Chequer Road during the last quarter of the nineteenth century and early years of the twentieth century. In the distance on the left are the British Schools, built in 1906 and opened by Mayor George Smith. Demolition occurred around 2009 and the site is currently being redeveloped.

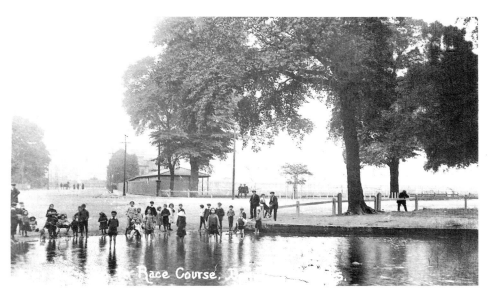

Pointing his camera in an easterly direction, Simonton has captured the 'Horseshoe Pond' with Bawtry Road off to the right and Grandstand Road straight ahead. Many local Edwardian photographic firms frequently reproduced this view on picture postcards and it was only natural that Simonton should do the same. During the eighteenth and nineteenth centuries, Doncaster's drinking water was pumped from the River Cheswold to a reservoir at the top of Hall Gate. The excess water eventually drained into the 'Horseshoe Pond' or 'Common Pond' pictured here. By the mid-1920s, the pond had disappeared in the extension of Carr House Road.

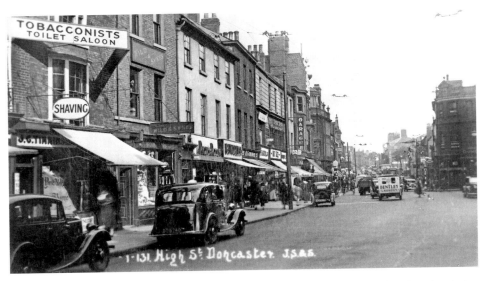

Simonton has placed his camera in the midst of busy High Street traffic and taken this view facing south, looking towards the junction with Hall Gate. To the left are the business premises of J. G. Timmins & Co. (tobacconists and gentlemen's hairdressers), Wild & Sykes (ironmongers) and Rhodes & Rosslynn. Timmins & Co. claimed most of their customers were regular callers and a wide range of smokers' accessories, including pipes, cigarette cases, holders, tobacco pouches, lighter, tobacco jars, and fancy match boxes, was always displayed at both their High Street and Sunny Bar premises. The firm's hairdressing section was alleged to have been among the finest equipped in the district.

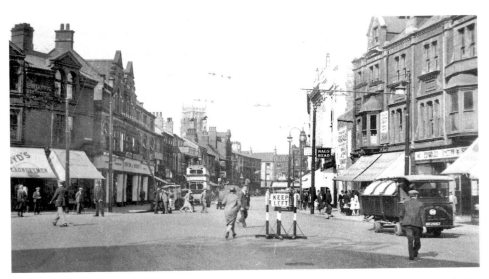

St Sepulchre Gate is depicted facing east with Clock Corner in the distance. The picture was probably taken around 1930 when the Nag's Head public house, on the right, was being rebuilt as one of the last stages of the St Sepulchre Gate widening scheme. To the left is the new building of Hodgson & Hepworth's, rebuilt following the fire in January 1901. The premises were built by local builder J. Sprakes & Sons to the designs of architects Athron & Beck. The property was demolished for the second phase of the Arndale (now French Gate) Centre's construction. One of the first trolleybuses to be used by the Doncaster Corporation can be seen in the photograph.

The Palace Theatre in Silver Street opened on
Monday 28 August 1911. It was built by local
builders Arnold & Son to the designs of Ward &
Ball. The theatre changed to motion pictures in
1920. The premises became known as the Essoldo
from 1937, surviving until 24 November 1962.
Thereafter the building was demolished and the
site redeveloped.

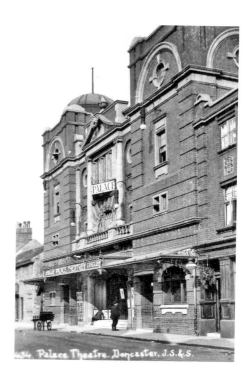

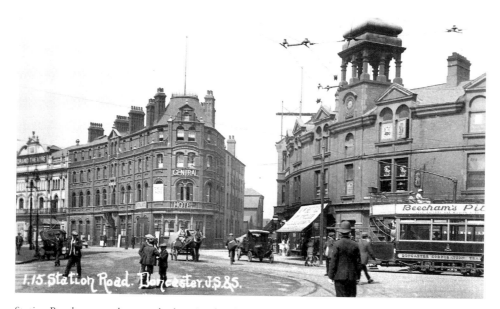

Station Road was another popular location for photographers producing postcard views, and Simonton
has captured the scene marvellously. Station Road was opened in 1882 and the work was financed
by both the Doncaster Corporation and the Great Northern Railway Company. The Central Hotel
was built by the Revd Edward Carr Glyn in 1890 as a Temperance hotel and café. Around 1918 the
property was bought by the YMCA and became known as the 'Central Hotel'. Currently the only
building standing is the Grand Theatre, to the left, built around 1899; the remaining buildings were
demolished during the 1970s.

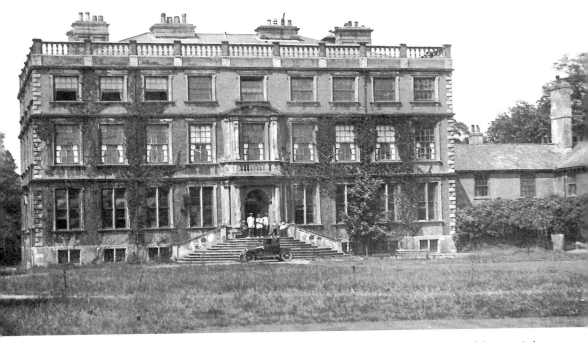

Wheatley Hall, built around 1683, was the seat of the Cooke family until the early years of the twentieth century. The park extended over 103 acres. On 30 May 1913, the *Doncaster Chronicle* reported that suffragists had attempted to blow up the untenanted Wheatley Hall but had failed. Around 1914, the Hall, together with the estate, was leased by Sir William Cooke to the Wheatley Golf Club. Sections of the Hall were converted to flats and another portion was used by the golf club as its club house. This ceased around 1930, when the golf club moved to an alternative site and the Hall was demolished. An idea of the Hall's former position was given in the company magazine *International Harvester Round*: 'Wheatley Hall was situated in a position roughly corresponding to the site of the present Implement Sales Warehouse, at the extreme western end of the Doncaster International Harvester complex.'

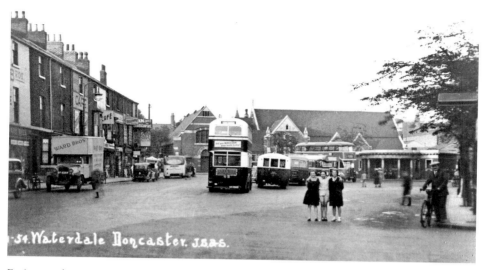

Facing north-east, Simonton has captured a section of Waterdale at a time when the properties on the left were changing from residential to commercial use and the area in front became a small bus terminus. Waterdale may be traced back to a deed of 1535 and by 1814 was a venue for horse sales, and the name 'Horse Fair' became attached to the area. But in 1882, 'Horse Fair' was dropped in favour of a return to Waterdale. The properties on the left, stretching between Young Street and Wood Street, were built by Mathias Harwood around 1826 and titled Harwood Terrace. Over the years much of this has been taken over by house furnishers Ward Bros, whose van is visible in the photograph.

Dunscroft

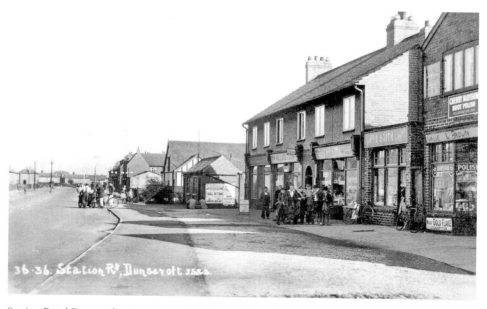

Station Road Dunscroft extends from High Street, Hatfield to Church Road, Stainforth. Amongst the commercial premises identified on the right are those belonging to R. Wallace & Son; L. & A. Eccles; D. Booth; and L. Brown. A poster right of centre advertises feature films showing at Stainforth Cinema.

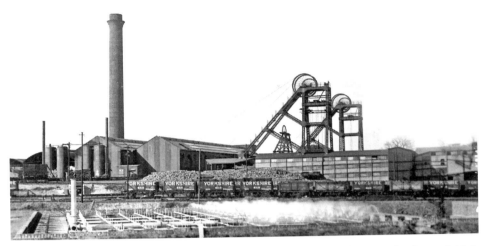

Simonton was operating at a time when nearly all the Doncaster area pits began production, and this is an early picture of Edlington colliery, which was known as Yorkshire Main. Sinking had begun there in December 1909 and was completed in July 1911. Operations were undertaken by the Staveley Coal & Iron Company. During the miners' strike of 1984/5, some ugly clashes between pickets and police were witnessed. Not long after the dispute, production men worked the last shift on Friday 11 October 1985; the site has been redeveloped. A memorial to the men of Yorkshire Main and their families was erected in December 1991.

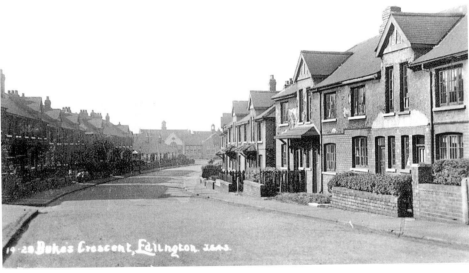

The *Doncaster Chronicle*, 2 August 1912, said that the colliery company at Edlington, with whom the Edlington Land & Development Company were under agreement to supply several hundred houses within a stipulated period, had made a demand for still a hundred more to be put in hand without delay. This meant that over the months ahead there would be between four and five hundred houses either occupied or in the process of completion. The New Edlington was to be laid out on 'Model Village' lines. One of the new streets was Duke's Crescent, extending from Maine Avenue to Church Road.

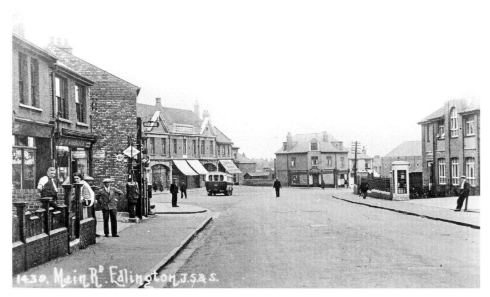

The *Doncaster Chronicle*, 2 August 1912, explained that the streets in New Edlington were of satisfactory width, radiating from a spacious main avenue on the 'boulevard' principal. '[The] houses are built in blocks of four or six, with plenty of air space between them, and there is provision for two recreation grounds and a smaller "village green". The shops are massed in the centre, looking on to Edlington Lane, which is now in the course of widening and macadamising, and already the Doncaster Co-operative Society has two excellent shops built and [trading].' In the top picture, looking north-east, the Co-operative building may be seen left of centre. The bottom picture shows commercial premises at the Edlington Lane/Main Avenue junction and they include grocer and confectioner A. Spargo, and Hutchinson, the tobacconist.

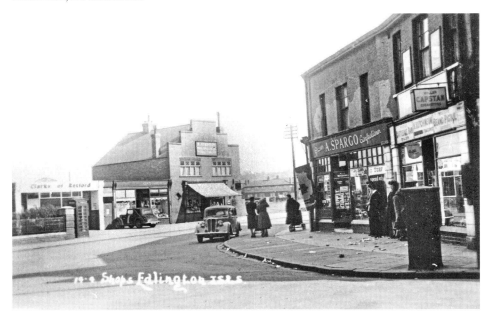

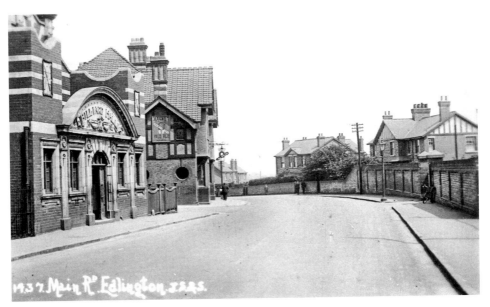

'The "York" Hotel at the entrance to the village, is in the course of erection … and plans are being prepared for a handsome Mission church under the direction of the Coalfields Church Extension Committee,' said the *Doncaster Chronicle* of 2 August 1912. It was also stated that a large area of farm land had been secured on the southern side of Edlington Lane for future extension and it was expected that the New Edlington Village would contain not less than 1,200 houses, with a population of about 6,000 people. 'The whole of these operations are under the control of the Edlington Freehold Land and Development Company, whose local surveyor was John Simmons of High Street, Doncaster,' said the newspaper. The photograph has been taken looking down Edlington Lane with the York Hotel off-centre to the left.

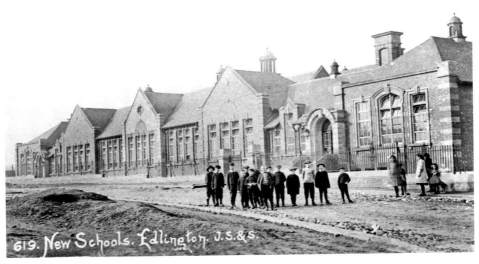

Edlington Victoria Road School at the junction of Victoria Road and Prince's Crescent was built in 1913 at a cost of over £11,000. The *Doncaster Chronicle* of 27 June 1913 stated that the school at the centre of the New Edlington Village was built on the quadrangle principle with the school buildings arranged on four sides of a square, and in the centre was a lawn.

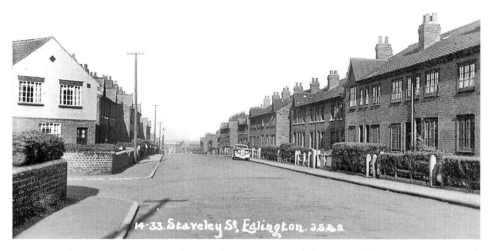

A notice in the *Doncaster Gazette* of 19 April 1914 announced that New Edlington was a place with a big future: 'Breezy, Bracing, Bright Invigorating. Situated some 400 feet above sea level, this model village is undoubtedly Doncaster's highest and healthiest suburb.' Staveley Street, seen here, extends from Edlington Lane to Prince's Crescent.

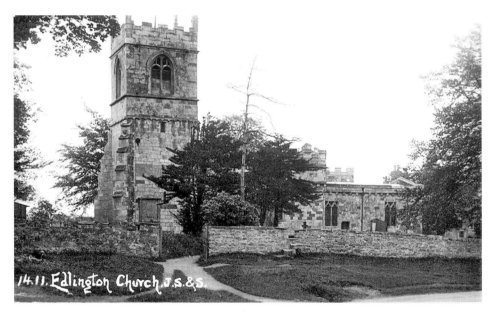

The stone-built church of St Peter in the old Edlington village is in the Perpendicular style with some remains of Norman work. It was repaired around 1878 and consists of chancel, nave, north aisle, south porch and an embattled western tower with pinnacles. The font dates from 1590 and the register 1731. On www.visitchurches.org.uk it is mentioned that 'after suffering years of uncertainty and vandalism, this lovely building was the first church to be vested in the Trust in 1971'. The website also adds that 'we were established by the 1968 Pastoral Measure: Ecclesiastical, Church of England law which is also approved by Parliament, and we celebrated our fortieth birthday in 2009. For over forty years, we've played a unique role in national life. Without us, over 340 irreplaceable historic buildings might have disappeared entirely. Instead many have once again become the focus of active community life.'

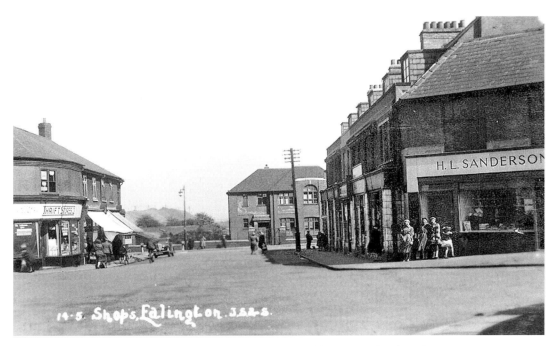

Simonton is standing in the middle of Main Avenue with Wellington Road to the right, Prince's Crescent to the left and Edlington Lane straight ahead. Harold Sanderson, whose premises are on the right, came to Edlington from Holmfirth around 1920 and established a thriving family butcher's business. He also supplied meat to schools in the area. In 1949, Harold's son Robert joined him in the business. Harold retired in the late 1950s, and died in 1968. Robert closed the business around 1962.

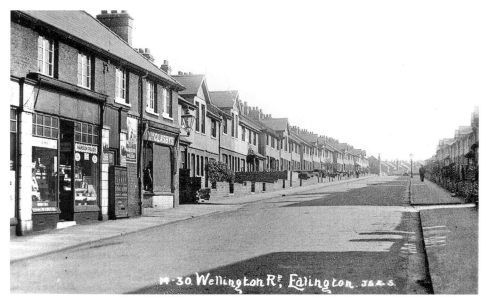

Wellington Road stretches between Maine Avenue and Gordon Road, and there is evidence to support the assumption that Simonton photographed almost every Edlington Street not long after it was built.

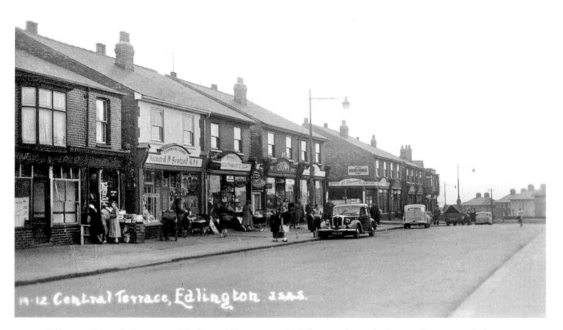

Edlington Lane facing east with Central Terrace on the left. Noted people from Edlington include Joe Harvey (Newcastle United's longest-serving captain and manager), Ron Flowers (a member of England's victorious 1966 World Cup squad) and Baron Lord Kirkham (Executive Chairman of DFS Furniture Company Ltd, and one of South Yorkshire's richest men).

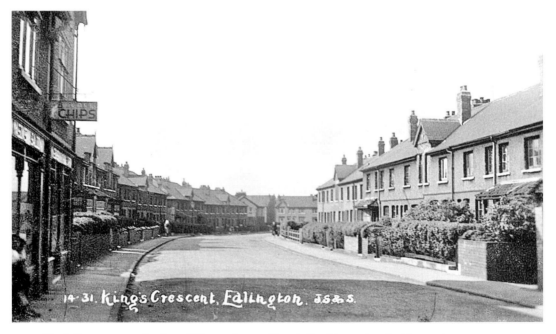

King's Crescent extending from Edlington Lane to Victoria Road is seen here looking north-west.

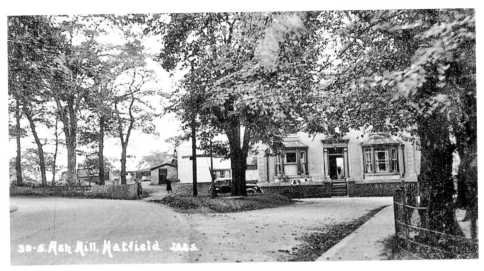

Ash Hill facing west with Doncaster road to the left and Ash Hill road to the right. According to Magilton (1977), Ash Hill Cottage, a two-bay cement-rendered building, off-centre to the right, maybe dates from the early nineteenth century. It is currently named Hatfields and is part of the Manor Road conservation area.

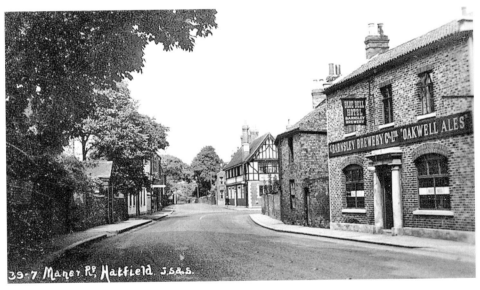

Simonton is positioned in Manor Road, with the Blue Bell public house and High Street (further along) to the right and Station Road and the Ingram Arms public house straight ahead. The Ingram Arms, dating back to at least 1796, was rebuilt in the 'Brewer's Tudor' style of pub architecture in 1922. The Blue Bell, an L-shaped cement-rendered building, may be traced to at least 1796. Besides the Barnsley Brewery Company, other owners have included Thomas Tune and James Fox & Sons. Magilton (1977) states that redevelopments at the core of Hatfield village have been minimal, with much of the modern expansion taking place mainly in the area west of Manor Road.

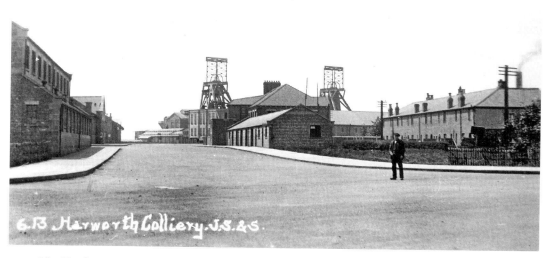

6.13 Harworth Colliery. J.S.&S.

The Northern Union Mining Company, an Anglo-German syndicate, began work on sinking Harworth colliery in 1913 but was impounded by HM Government following the interruptions of the First World War. Thereafter the Harworth Main Colliery Co. Ltd took control, and the sinking of a new shaft, begun in June 1919, was completed in December 1923. The colliery was later taken over by Barber, Walker & Co. Ltd and bought by R. J. Budge in 1994. In recent times the colliery has been mothballed. On www.minersadvice. co.uk it is stated that 'to the uninitiated Harworth is to all intents and purposes a Doncaster pit, sitting as it does just over the fields from Rossington and a few miles from Doncaster. It is however a Nottingham pit, its workforce much more strongly inclined to the dominant moderate traditions of that coalfield rather than the "red ragging" pit culture of Doncaster. Being on the border of both traditions it has been the storm centre of internal political and trade union struggle on a number of occasions.'

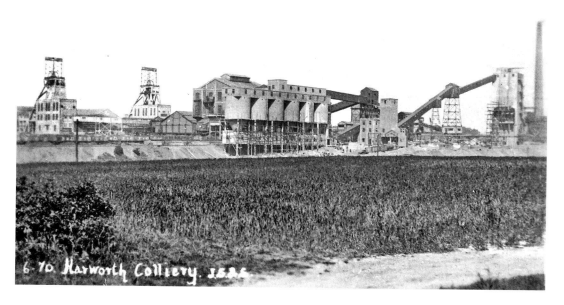

6.10 Harworth Colliery. J.S.&S.

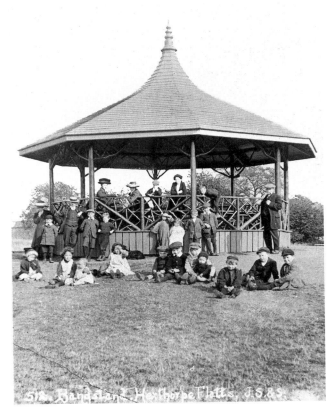

512. Bandstand Hexthorpe Flatts, J.S.&S.

In 1850 Doncaster Corporation planned to convert the Hexthorpe Flatts into a public pleasure ground. Sir Robert Paxton, who designed Chatsworth House gardens, was approached but he declined. He said the time was not right and that the Corporation should first look at two other requirements for the town, the cemetery and the improvement of the water works. This advice was taken and so the development of the Flatts was delayed for another fifty-two years. Frank Pearson (1991) states that during June 1902, the work to convert the area into a recreation area included sloping the quarry walls, making a tea house, building a bandstand, providing toilets, and planting willows. The Flatts were 'thrown open to the public during the August bank holiday' and news reports state the event was attended by several thousand. The picture on the left shows the bandstand. while the one below shows the pavilion.

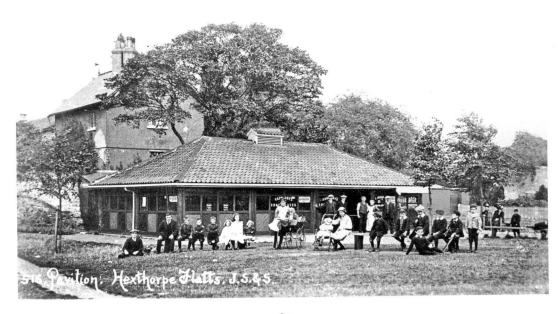

516. Pavilion, Hexthorpe Flatts. J.S.&S

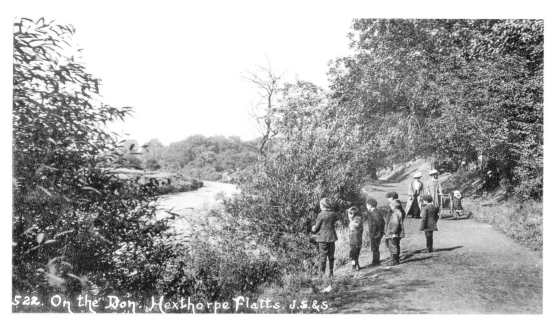

522. On the Don. Hexthorpe Flatts. J.S.&S.

In subsequent years the Flatts developed into a workable venture. A caretaker was appointed in 1906 and in time a park keeper. Boating on the river was also encouraged, a boat house was built and a roadway made to a landing stage. Around the same time a pavilion was erected for concerts and variety performances. Further expansion in the Flatts took place in the late 1920s. An area known as the Dell, which included, amongst other features, formal flower beds and rockeries, was opened in April 1929 and floodlit two years later. After enjoying immense success, with coachloads of visitors from around South Yorkshire, in subsequent years there was a decline in popularity and the river is no longer used for boating. But Hexthorpe Flatts still remains today a popular park. The area provided a wealth of postcard opportunities for many photographers, including Simonton. The top picture shows children by the river and the one below shows the rose garden in the Dell.

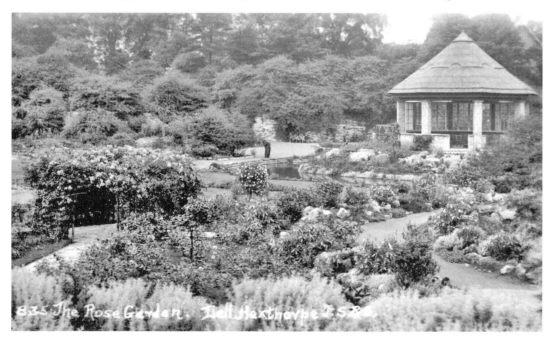

825. The Rose Garden. Dell. Hexthorpe J.S.&S.

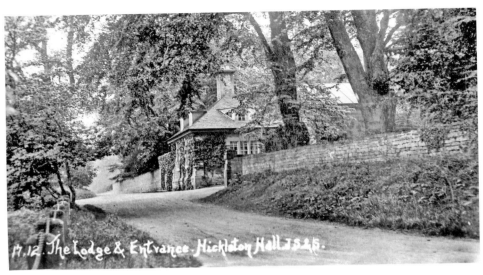

17.12. The Lodge & Entrance. Hickleton Hall 1526.

Magilton (1977) states that 'the surviving [Hickleton] estate wall, incorporate[s] stone mullion windows ... and appears to include part of the earlier hall designed by Smythson (?). Hickleton Hall itself [is] a mid-eighteenth-century structure.' The existing Hall was in fact designed by James Paine for Godfrey Wentworth in 1745–8. For a number of years, the Hall and Hickleton estate were owned by the Halifax family, but in the late 1940s they were acquired by the Sisters of the Order of the Holy Paraclete. In the early 1960s, the Hall was taken over as a Sue Ryder Home for European stateless persons. Later it became a nursing home. The Lodge and entrance are seen here looking south.

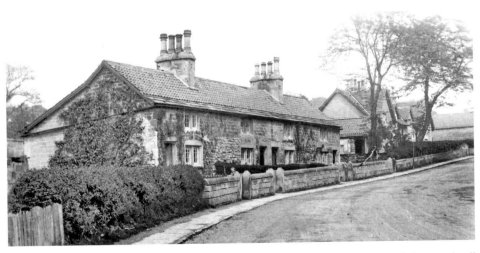

Hickleton's Doncaster Road, facing north, is seen here. Magilton (1977) mentioned that nearly all the cottages, which range in date from the seventeenth to the nineteenth centuries, are stonebuilt and present an attractive village-scape. The nearby church of St Wilfrid, begun in the twelfth century and completed in the fifteenth, was restored in 1876–88 by George Frederick Bodley, a pupil of George Gilbert Scott. After the Second World War, the Halifax family moved to Garraby near York, but they still own some of the land, houses and farms in Hickleton.

4

KIRK SANDALL TO STAINFORTH

KIRK SANDALL

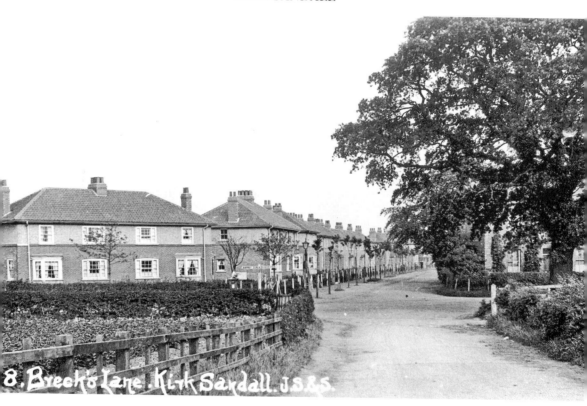

8. Breck's Lane. Kirk Sandall. J.S.&S.

Brecks Lane, viewed here, is a main arterial road linking Doncaster Road and Armthorpe Lane in Kirk Sandall. It was one of the first thoroughfares to be developed when St Helen's-based Pilkington Bros established a plate glass works and housing estate at Kirk Sandall during the early 1920s. The *Doncaster Gazette* of 9 April stated that the contract for the first portion of the new Kirk Sandall was placed with Doncaster's H. Arnold & Son and Johnson & Moore of Balby. New houses within the portion were to be situated near the vicarage and along Brecks Lane.

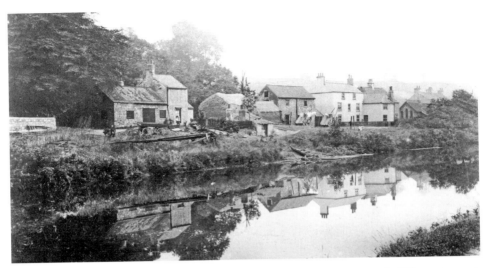

The name Levitt Hagg was probably first given to a clearing below the Warmsworth Cliffs, on the south bank of the River Don. The earliest known reference to the area is a rental paid in 1629. During the mid-eighteenth century, Levitt Hagg was adopted as the name for a dwelling house erected on part of the site of the clearing. Later, when more buildings were constructed and a small village was formed, Levitt Hagg was used for the name of the whole settlement. Nos 1 and 2 Levitt Hagg can be seen in this view looking south-west from the north side of the River Don.

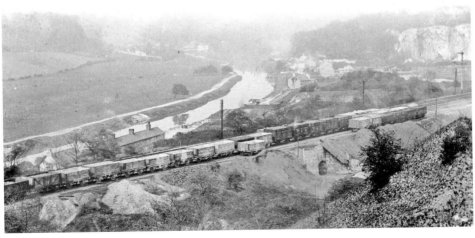

From the middle of the eighteenth century, virtually all the land in Warmsworth, including the Cliffs, was in the possession of two families, the Batties and the Aldams. John Battie began quarrying operations at the base of the Warmsworth Cliffs in the 1750s. He had entered the quarrying business because the growth in population in the eighteenth century had created a demand for stone to build more houses. The increase in population also led to higher food prices and a need for more food growing areas. This in turn initiated the establishment of lime-burning at the quarries, as lime was essential in the reclamation of marginal land for agriculture.

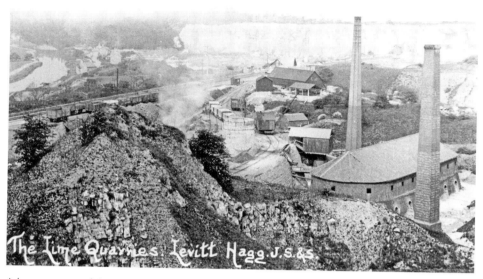

A large amount of the output at Levitt Hagg was distributed by boat, but when the South Yorkshire Railway Company's line was extended through the Warmsworth Cliffs in 1849, it enabled a considerable proportion of the stone and lime to be conveyed by rail. Quarrying operations can be seen in this view and the one on the previous page; both are looking in a north-easterly direction.

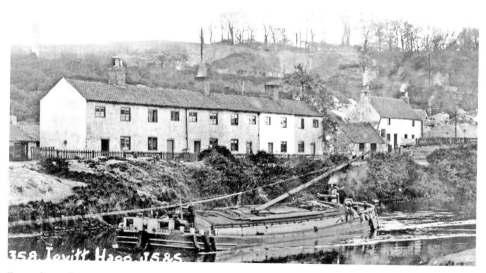

From the early nineteenth century, Joseph Lockwood, Robert Kemp and William Blagden paid an annual rent of £600 for use of the quarries, associated land and buildings. Thereafter the village of Levitt Hagg began to grow and so did the business as more quarries in the Warmsworth Cliffs were leased. By 1850 the annual figure from all the quarries was quoted as 13,000 tons of lime and 22,000 tons of stone. Pictured is a group of six cottages, known as White Row; these were erected by Messrs Lockwood, Blagden & Crawshaw around 1815. Each of the cottages contained one living room, two bedrooms and a pantry beneath the staircase.

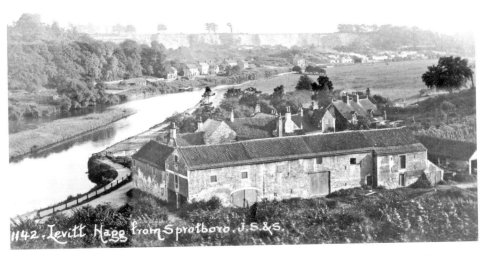

More houses were built at Levitt Hagg during 1875, and to meet the needs for worship and recreation, a Mission Hall and Reading Room were erected in 1878. During 1925 a County Medical Officer made a report on the sanitary conditions at Levitt Hagg. The poor conditions and the seriously polluted state of the nearby river led to all the houses being condemned as unfit for occupation and by 1957 the area was cleared. Also, the introduction of modern machinery at the Warmsworth Cliff quarries in the late 1930s had reduced the workforce and also lessened the housing requirement at the village.

LOVERSALL

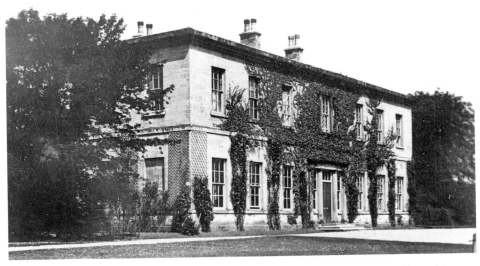

Patricia Seddon in *Loversall* (1972) gives details of the old Loversall Hall and the building of the new one: 'George Augustus was the last occupant of the old Hall ... [he and his wife] came to Loversall, but he died suddenly, 5 May 1808, aged twenty-eight. In 1808, the demolition of the old Loversall Hall began. The new Hall took three years to build for [James] Fenton took up residence in 1811 and remained until 1816.'

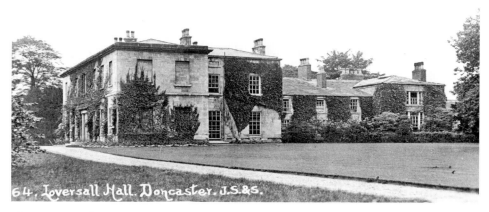

The new Loversall Hall is T-shaped, and constructed of limestone ashlars. The kitchen garden is held to be the site of the previous Hall, and buried foundations are said to occupy much of the area. A dovecote in the north-east corner of the garden dates from the late sixteenth to seventeenth century and probably accompanied the previous Hall. Fenton was succeeded by a number of tenants, until the Skipwith family arrived at Loversall in the 1890s and remained there until the late 1960s. Subsequent occupants have included Malcolm Colbear, who used the premises to house his nationally acclaimed advertising agency.

MEXBOROUGH

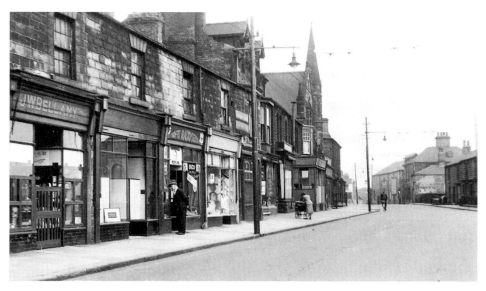

Bank Street looking east, with the Wesleyan Church in the centre. The church was built in 1904, and the *South Yorkshire Times* of 29 October 1904 reported that 'the new Wesleyan Church is situated immediately opposite the old chapel on the site once occupied by the Old Don Pottery and its erection has filled up a gap in Bank Street which has always been an eye-sore … The new buildings are designed in the late Gothic style, freely treated with foliated ornamentation … the building, exclusive of the cost of the land and the architects fees, has cost £3,950. Messrs John Wills & Sons of Denby and London are the architects … The contractors were Messrs Charles Sprakes & Sons of Doncaster.'

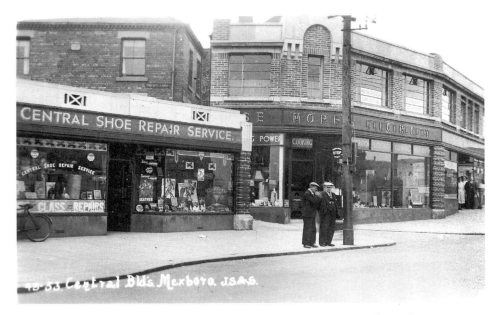

Throughout the eighteenth, nineteenth and much of the twentieth centuries Mexborough's economy was based around coal mining, quarrying, brickworks and the production of ceramics, and it soon became a busy railway junction. Following the demise of the coal mining industry in the 1980s, Mexborough, like many ex-mining South Yorkshire towns and villages, is still in the process of economic and social recovery. Central Buildings, situated at the junction of Bank Street/Adwick Road/Doncaster Road, is seen here with figures posing in the doorway of an electrical store.

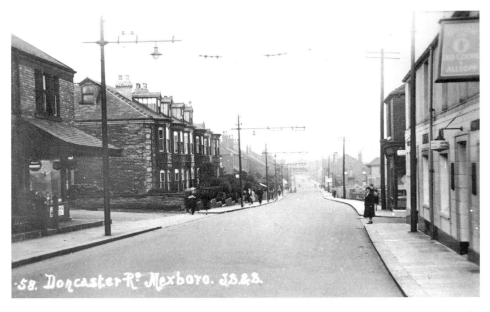

View looking north-east along Doncaster Road in the trolleybus era, with the Union Inn on the right. The inn dated from at least 1869 (*Doncaster Gazette*, 26 November 1869) and closed on 30 July 1967 (*South Yorkshire Times*, 29 July 1967). Past owners included William Henry Jones Mill; Inde Coope; and Allsopp Ltd.

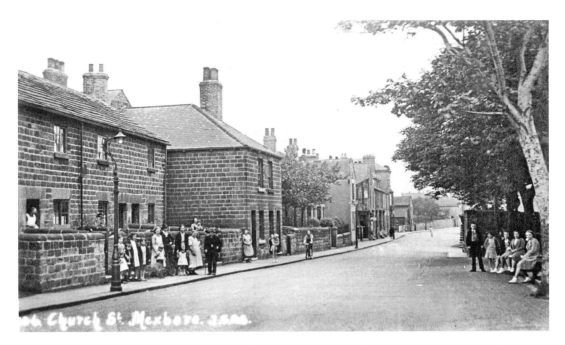

Simonton has set up his camera in the middle of Church Street and is facing east for this view, taken before 1930. After this time many properties on the left were demolished. Out of view behind the trees on the right is the Ferry Boat Inn.

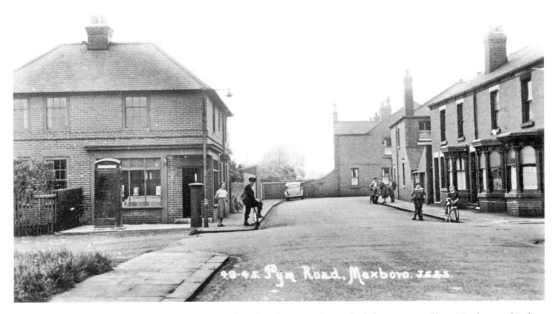

Pym Road stretches between Albert Road and Milton Road. On the left is a post office. Mexborough's first post office was opened in Hirstgate, off Doncaster Road, on 29 October 1857, although there was a receiving office noted in the town in 1852.

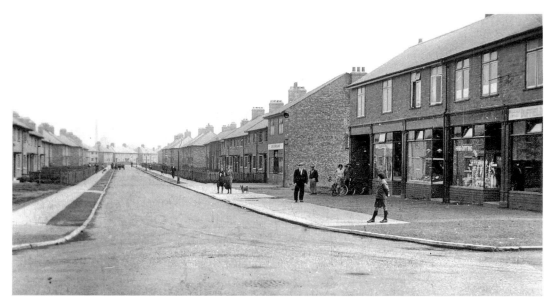

The *Doncaster Gazette* of 24 April 1908 reported that the entire outlook at Thorne was revolutionised as the result of a bed of coal of good thickness being found at a workable depth at Moorends. The place where the boring operations had been carried out was about 1½ miles from Thorne, on the road leading to Goole. After many trials and tribulations in the post-war years, the shafts were completed during 1926, seventeen years after the commencement of sinking operations. The *Doncaster Gazette* of 8 May 1925 informed that the Housing Corporation of Great Britain Ltd of London had secured the contract for the first instalment of the new colliery village at Moorends. The contract was for 250 houses of various types, which were to be built to the plans and designs of Harold E. Jarvis, chief architect to Messrs Pease and Partners Ltd, of Darlington, the proprietors of the colliery. Alexandra Road is seen in the top picture; Micklethwaite Road in the bottom one.

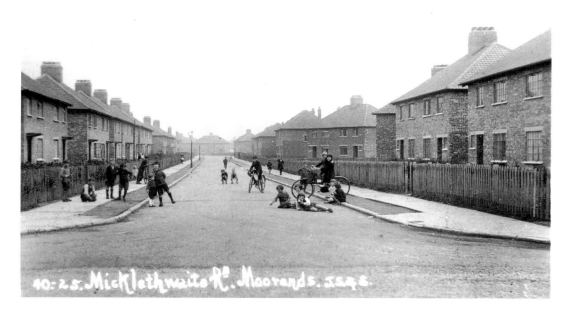

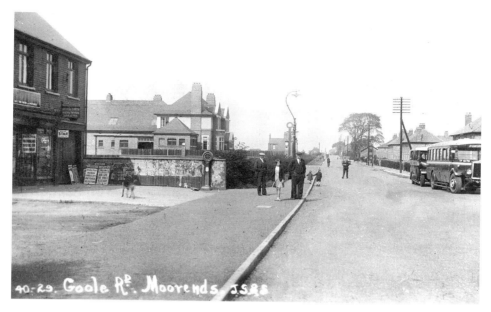

Architect Jarvis told the *Doncaster Gazette* of 8 May 1925 that 'the colliery village adjoins the road from Thorne to Marshland, and is to be laid out on Town Planning lines, and one of the points to be borne in mind is that the dwellers in the new village shall not be constantly reminded of the colliery's existence. The housing site proper is planned on "radial" lines. There will be an avoidance of long, monotonous, parallel roads, and the building lines will be broken and the various types of houses distributed in such a way as to give variety to the aspect of the village. When completed the village will have from 1,800 to 2,000 houses. The majority of the houses would probably be of the non-parlour type with three bedrooms ... All the houses will be equipped with bathrooms and will be electrically lighted.' Goole Road is seen in the top picture and Northgate in the one below.

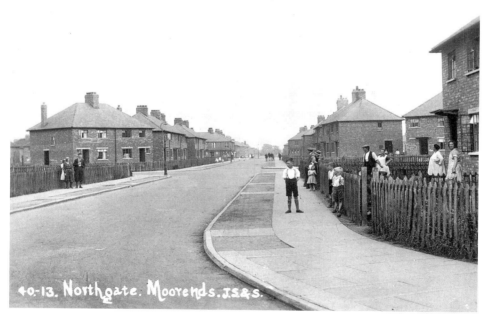

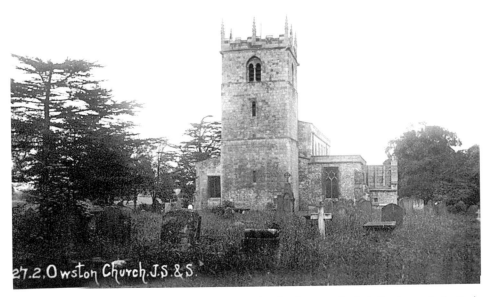

The Church of All Saints at Owston stands on the north side of Owston Park. Built of stone in the Early English and Perpendicular styles, it consists of chancel, clerestoried nave, two side chapels, south porch and an embattled tower of the Early English period with pinnacles. The chancel, Early English, retains a pre-Reformation stone altar and some remains of a canopied tomb of the fourteenth century. In the church are several monuments to the Cooke family. The chancel was completely restored in 1872 and 1873, under the direction of Sir G. Gilbert Scott RA at the expense of P. T. Davies-Cooke. The cost of the work was over £2,000. In 1898 the tower was restored at a cost of £700. The register dates from 1683.

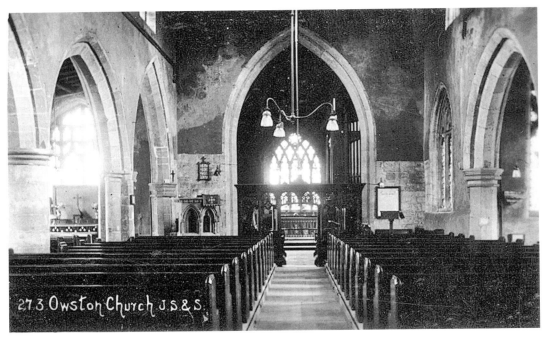

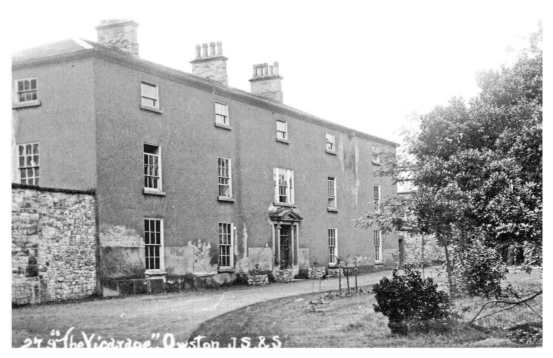

Magilton (1977) says that practically nothing survives of Owston village older than estate cottages and the Hall. Owston was designated a conservation area on 15 June 1970 and it is made up of sixteen listed structures, including the Grade I listed Church of All Saints and Grade II* listed Hall. On www.doncaster.gov. uk it is stated that 'there is a compact arrangement of dwellings and former barns and outbuildings to the area north of the hall and the adjoining Church of All Saints, with several former lodges along the boundary of the former estate'. Owston vicarage is seen in the top picture and the Gate Lodge in the one below.

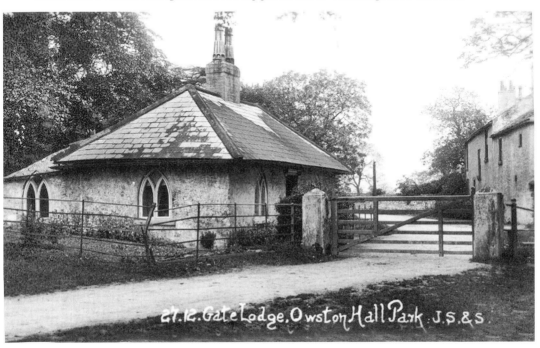

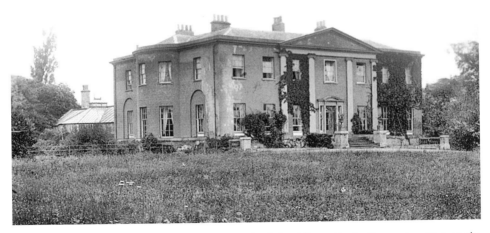

Owston Hall was built in the late eighteenth century by Colonel Bryan Cooke. Pevsner (1958) states the house was designed by William Porden. However, whilst Porden prepared some designs for Owston these were never carried out. Instead, William Lindley undertook additions and alterations at Owston in 1794. The grounds of Owston Hall were landscaped by Humphrey Repton in the late eighteenth century. For many years, the Owston Hall and estate was owned by successive generations of the Davies-Cooke family. But, under the heading 'Hall's New Role' the *Doncaster Chronicle* of 14 March 1935 announced that Owston Hall, the home of the Davies- Cooke family for centuries, had been converted into flats. In spite of several changes of use during the twentieth century, Owston Hall still survives intact today.

PICKBURN

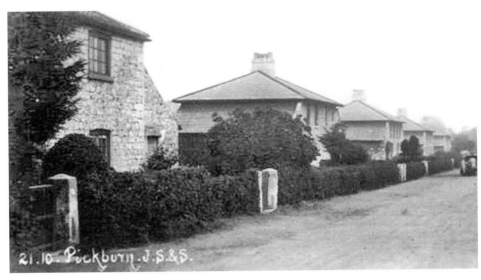

Brodsworth and Pickburn villages are adjacent to each other and belonged to the old Brodsworth Estate. A railway, forming part of the Denaby Branch, passed through Pickburn, and latterly was mainly used for coal traffic. There also existed a Pickburn-and-Brodsworth railway station. For this view Simonton is facing east, looking along Pickburn Lane. Although not in the Brodsworth conservation area, some of the properties of Pickburn are of interest and three are listed Grade II.

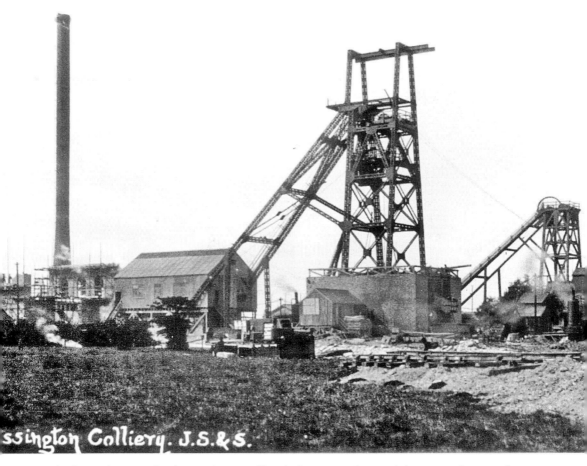

ssington Colliery. J.S.& S.

The first sod was cut for the Rossington colliery in June 1912. It was a joint venture between the Sheepbridge Coal & Iron Co. and Messrs John Brown & Co. Shafts No. 1 and 2 were completed in 1915 and the first coal was brought up in that year. This picture is another example of Simonton being fully aware of colliery developments in the Doncaster area and is an early view of the Rossington workings. In 1969, Coalite opened a foundry at Rossington to produce coke. The 1984/85 strike was marked by ugly scenes at the colliery, with picketers clashing with police and management. The colliery closed for a period in 1993 but was taken over by RJB Mining in 1994. Production ceased in 2006 and the colliery site has been cleared awaiting redevelopment.

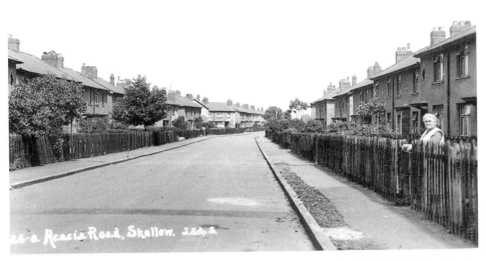

Acacia Road extends from Crossfield Lane and formed part of an estate built by Adwick Urban District Council during the late 1920s. The building venture was an attempt to meet the continuing housing demand for Bullcroft colliery miners and included some 120 properties.

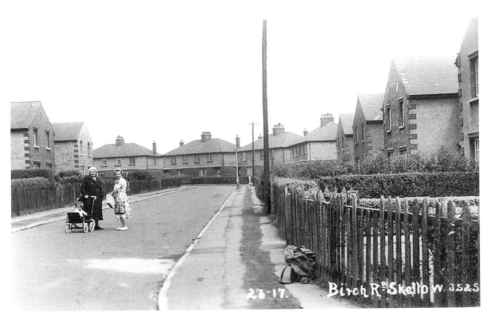

Simonton has named this street Birch Road, but it is really Birch Avenue, extending in a horseshoe from Hawthorne Crescent. It also provides access to Elm Road. Birch Road was built by Adwick Urban Council around 1919, along with Briar Road and Beech Road, and included sixtyfive pairs of semi-detached houses.

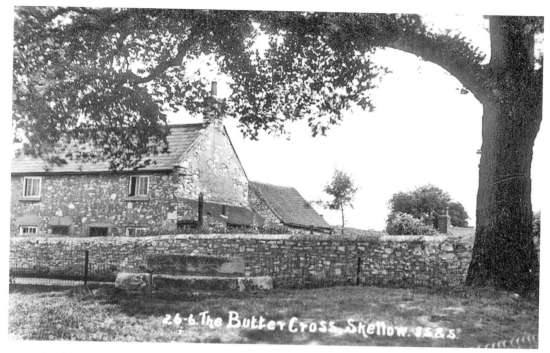

An idyllic portrait of Skellow is painted by the *Doncaster Chronicle* of 22 June 1961: 'A hundred years ago, Skellow had its own Market Day, where around the Butter Cross, farmers' wives brought their produce of eggs, butter, cheese, etc., for sale and women from surrounding villages walked two or three miles to purchase them … The farms at Skellow made their own cheeses, and the old-fashioned heavy stone cheese presses may still be seen lying about. The old village had a large maltkiln, where the barley malt was turned each day – it had to be to reach the best condition – with large wooden shovels on a concrete floor. The constant friction of wood on concrete produced a surface like glass, and there the village dances took place, say at the Village Feast, Harvest Home, Christmas, etc.' The Skellow Butter Cross is seen in the top picture; the picture below shows a house opposite the Butter Cross out of view to the right.

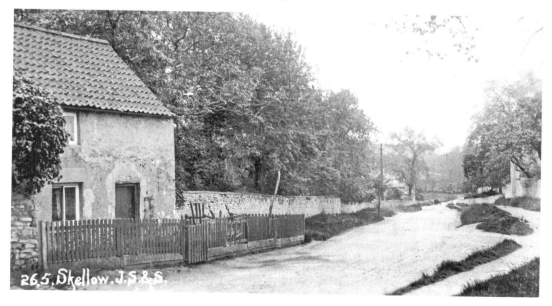

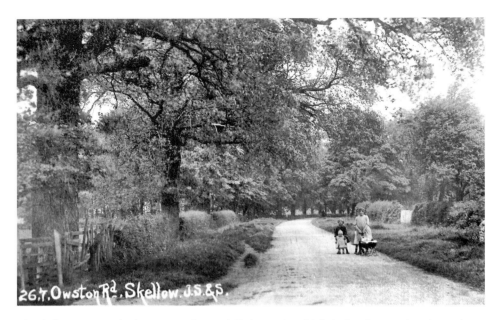

The Skellow name is of Viking origin; the word 'Skel' meaning chieftain. But the name has changed over the years and was known as 'Scanhalla' in 1086, 'Skelehall' in 1203, 'Skellawe' in 1379, and Skellow in 1493. Curiously, while Skellow has had some interesting features over the centuries, it has never had a church of its own, within its own boundaries. Its place of worship was a good mile away at Owston, where the chief landlord and squire resided. Simonton has located this picture at Skellow when it is really at Carcroft, showing Owston Road, extending from Carcroft High Street to Lodge Road.

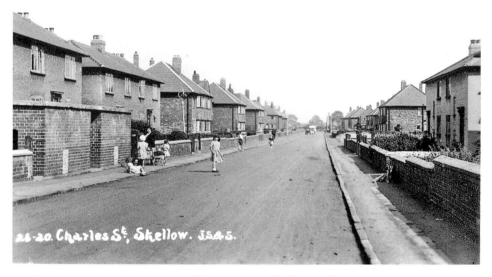

Besides the Adwick Urban Council building houses at Skellow for Bullcroft miners, large numbers were also constructed by the Industrial Housing Association Ltd. Houses built at Skellow formed New Skellow, and some of the streets were named after British kings. These included Charles Street, seen here, and stretching between Chestnut Avenue and Elm Road.

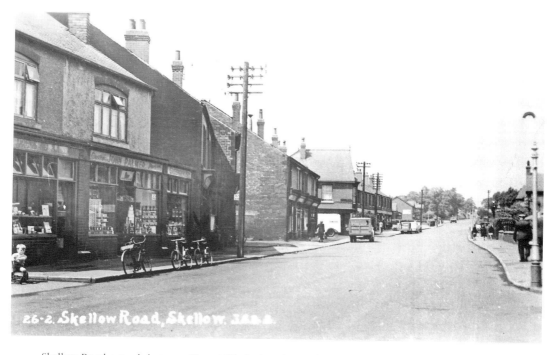

Skellow Road extends between Cross Hill, the junction with Owston Road/Station Road and Askern Road. This stretch of shops, (and a public house out of view further along) on the thoroughfare's southern side, was built during the 1920s. One of the traders identified in the top picture is grocer John Palmer. The picture below shows the premises of Tyler & Blanshard.

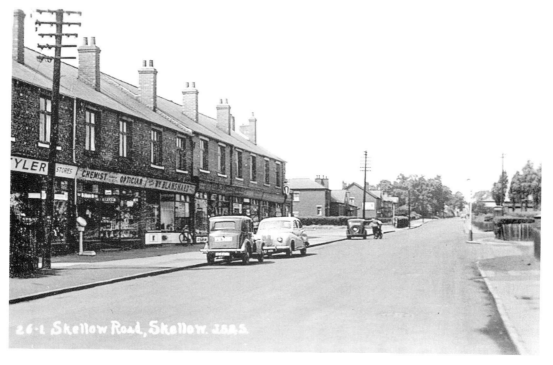

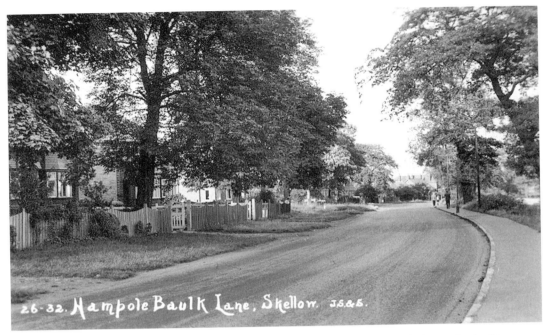

26-32. Hampole Baulk Lane, Skellow. J.S.&S.

Magilton (1977) is quite dismissive of both Carcroft and Skellow, stating that little remains in either village in the way of important standing monuments: 'Both are engulfed with pit housing ... In Skellow it should be possible to preserve the core of the old village, centred on the Market Cross ... Neither has a medieval church.'

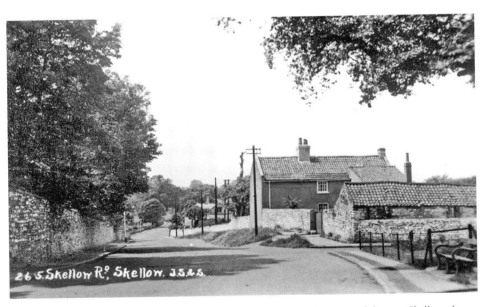

26 5.Skellow R°, Skellow. J.S.&S.

The *Doncaster Chronicle* of 15 June 1961 stated: 'During the development of the new Skellow, due to the advent of Bullcroft Colliery, skeletons were found in the gutter along the roadway, each one having by its side the remains of some implement of warfare. One was a lance, another was a spear, resting beside the bones. It is not difficult to imagine that these were the remains of Cavaliers, fallen in conflict. Each [grave] was about two feet six inches deep.'

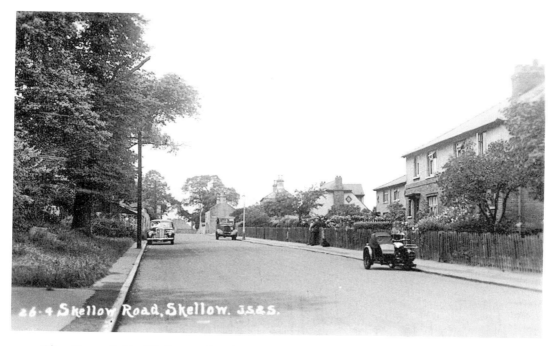

26·4 Skellow Road, Skellow. J.S.&S.

Oliver Cromwell visited Skellow searching for an answer to an irritating, baffling problem. King Charles' Cavaliers had been passing through, both north and south, along the Great North Road, and had to be stopped if Cromwell was to have absolute domination of Britain. Consequently, General Fairfax, with 300 soldiers, was despatched to Doncaster. Yet, after about four months, Fairfax received reliable reports that Cavaliers were successfully bypassing the town. Cromwell decided that he needed to investigate the problem in more detail. So, he stayed for five days in Doncaster. For both these photographs Simonton is standing in Skellow Road facing west.

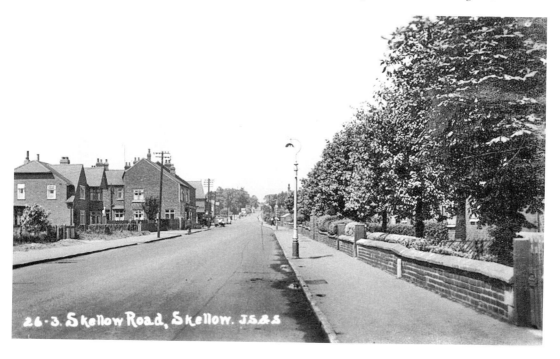

26·3 Skellow Road, Skellow. J.S.&S.

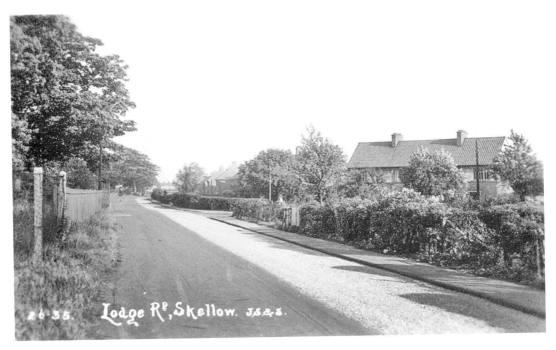

Lodge Road extends between Crossfield Road and Owston Lane.

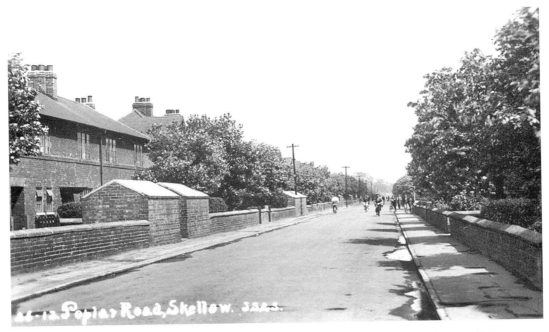

Poplar Road, a long thoroughfare built in New Skellow during the 1920s, stretches north-east between Skellow Road and Lodge Road. Bullcroft colliery closed in 1970 and it has been said that demographic evidence of the former mining community is evident in Skellow in both higher-than-average levels of unemployment and a strong sense of community, with residents knowing their neighbours and those that live around them.

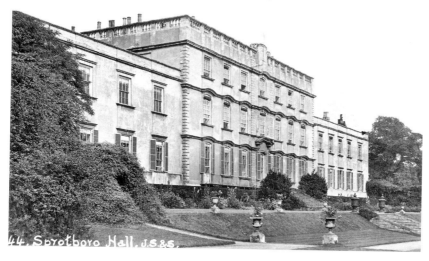

Sprotbrough Hall was built by Sir Godfrey Copley around 1685 and may have replaced an older house that had existed nearer the church. The Hall sat comfortably amid formal gardens in the Dutch and French style, and commanded a wide view of the surrounding countryside. Sir Godfrey Copley died in 1709 and, because his son had predeceased him, the estate passed to Lionel Copley of Wadworth. The Copley's Sprotbrough reign finally came to an end during the early 1920s, when the property was sold to meet heavy death duties. The Hall's contents were sold in February 1926, and by mid-April the *Doncaster Gazette* was reporting that the demolition of Sprotbrough Hall was well underway.

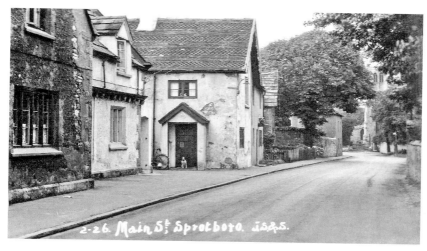

Properties on the north side of Main Street are featured here. The dwelling on the immediate left was Lot 55 at the Sprotbrough Estate sale. It is described as 'a capital semi-detached cottage … with southern aspect, stone built and slated, containing Two Bedrooms and Two Rooms down. Wash House, Yard, E. C. and Coals, Good Garden, in all about 23 poles … let to an Estate Servant on a Service Tenancy determinable with service'. Next door was Lot 56, listed as 'The Adjoining and Similar Cottage but with inside Closet, Good Garden, extending in all to about 17 poles'. This property too was 'let to an Estate Servant on a Service Tenancy determinable with service'.

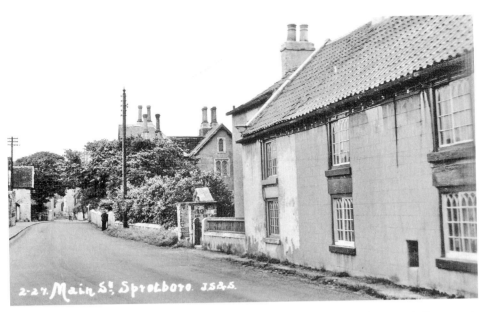

Main Street extends from Cadeby Road to Thorpe Lane. To take this top photograph Simonton is facing east with the church just visible on the left. On the right is Rambler's Cottage, and a village pump is off-centre to the left. The pump itself was situated beneath an impressive coat of arms in a stone alcove. Until the sale of the Copley estate in September 1925, all the properties in the village belonged to the family. Sprotbrough was designated a conservation area on 21 December 1970 and within the area there are six listed structures. Main Street is at the heart of the conservation area. A clear view of the Estate House is seen in the view below. It was Lot 46 in the sale catalogue and described as 'occupying a charming situation in the centre of the Village, substantially built of stone, cement faced and with a slated gabled roof, latticed windows and glazed porch ... Outside are Wash House, Meal House, Piggery, Motor shed and Coal House, the whole being enclosed in a delightful garden.'

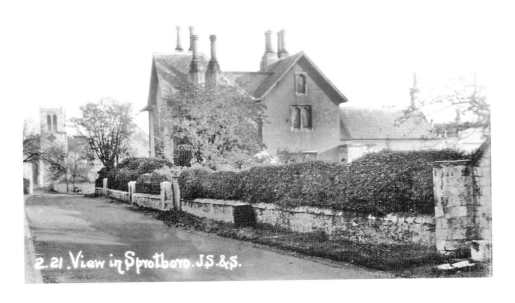

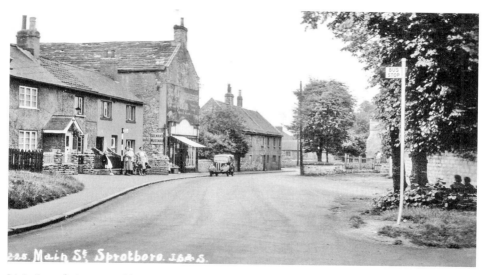

Main Street facing east, with St Mary's church out of view to the right. The terrace of three properties on the left was Lots 47 to 51 (inclusive) at the 1925 sale. The tall, gabled building was Lot 29a, described as 'a Charming Old-Fashioned Residence in capital order, known as Shire Farm ... having [a] long frontage to Thorpe Lane ... The Picturesque House suitable for a gentleman's occupation, situated in a Pretty Garden is stone built and slated and contains Four Bed Rooms, Two Box Rooms, Two Garretts, Bath room (h. And c.) and W. C ... ' The shop frontage was added after the sale and for a time the premises were known as Shire's Stores. Note the advertisement for the Scala Progressive Club on the gable end.

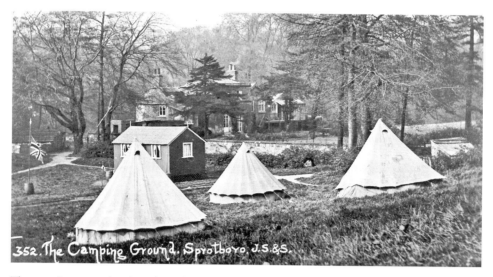

The camping ground at Sprotbrough on Whit Monday, 1914. The location is a field between the river and a bend in the road to Warmsworth. In the background is the old Flint Mill house. The first reference to a mill at Sprotbrough is in a charter of 1279. Thereafter the water of the Don powered mills at Sprotbrough for centuries. In *Sprotbrough in History Part Two*, it is recorded that the change from fulling to flint grinding took place around the end of the eighteenth century and that flint grinding continued until about 1880 – 'there is no record of the Flint Mill after 1877. The decline in trade at the Swinton potteries towards the last quarter of the nineteenth century spelt the doom of the Flint Mill.' The mill and house have since been demolished.

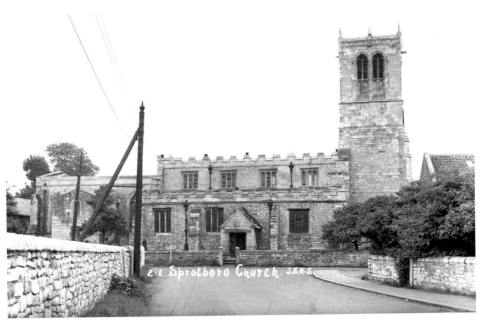

Sprotbrough's St Mary's church is late Norman and dates from around 1176. It is a Grade I listed building. On www.stmarys-sprotbrough.co.uk we are informed that 'the original church was almost certainly small with two cells (nave and chancel). It was narrow, tall and only two thirds the present length with a small and probably square chancel. The design was typical of Saxon and some early Norman churches. Since its foundation it has been radically altered. Today only traces of the masonry of Albreda's church remain. They are situated between the arches of the first two bays in the nave arcades. The church as we see it today is essentially as it would have been around 1520.' In 1516, the roof was replaced and clerestory windows inserted. The porch dates from 1632. Major restoration work took place in the church interior during 1914–15, when the chancel was restored and the pulpit altered, reusing the sixteenth- or seventeenth-century carved panels. The top picture shows the church from Thorpe Lane; the one below from Park Drive.

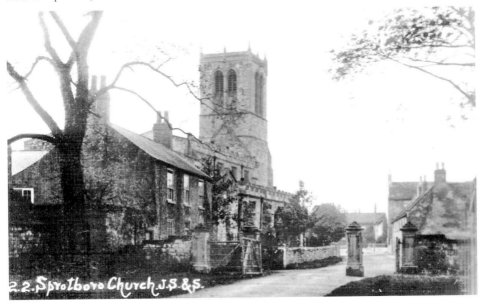

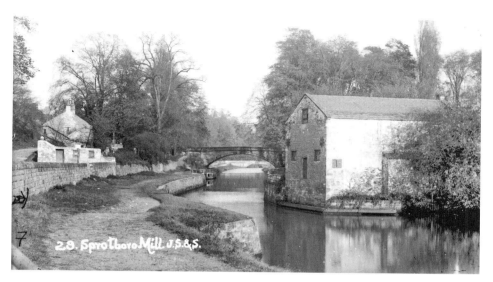

William Palmer's map of the River Don (1722) indicates the site of the corn mill pictured on the right facing east. But it is pointed out in *Sprotbrough in History Part Two* that 'a Deed of Feoffment (act of granting possession) was indented by Phillip Copley on 10 October 1546 – the property described in this indenture related to estates at Sprotbrough … and included four water mills'. White's Directory (1838) notes 'Edward Shepherd, corn Miller; 1864 Luke Crawshaw, Corn Miller'. Further entries for the mill are included in twentieth-century directories, but the *Doncaster Chronicle* of 24 June 1932 carried a picture of the mill being demolished. The stone bridge in the background was replaced by a steel structure in 1934.

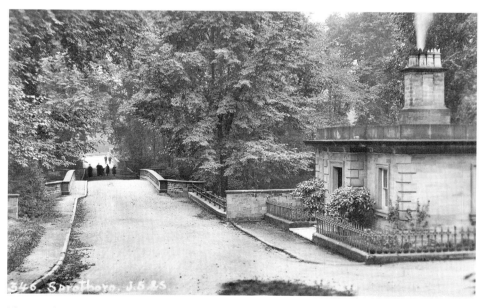

The Sprotbrough Bridge toll house on the north side of the River Don was photographed facing south. Until 1888, tolls were collected from this building for the repair and maintenance of the river and canal bridges. The Lodge was Lot 76 in the 1925 sale catalogue and was described as 'occupying a delightfully rural position at the Bridge Head, and adjoining Boat Lane. It is substantially built of dressed stone with flat roof with projecting eaves, and contains Four Rooms, Well of water and Garden, in all about 33 poles … let to Mr H. Birkinshaw, with other lands. Apportioned Rent £11 per annum.' The building is Grade II listed.

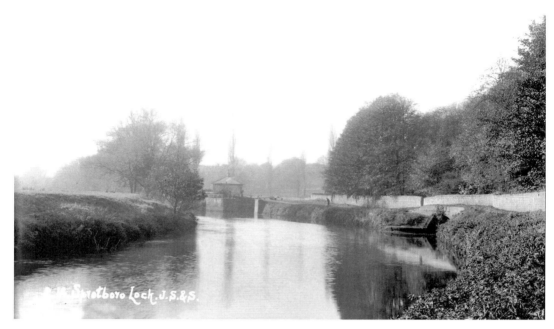

The River Don (also called *Dun* in some stretches) rises in the Pennines and flows for 70 miles (110 kilometres) eastwards, through the Don Valley, via Penistone, Sheffield, Rotherham, Mexborough, Conisbrough, Sprotbrough, Doncaster and Stainforth. Navigation to Sheffield was made possible by the construction of weirs, locks and canal cuttings to avoid circuitous and unnavigable sections. In 1980 Sprotbrough lock was rebuilt by the Sheffield & South Yorkshire Navigation as part of a £17 million improvement scheme, which aimed to make Rotherham accessible to craft carrying up to 700 tons via Goole and the new Junction Canal. The Sprotbrough work cost approximately £98,000 and was completed in eleven months. The new lock was opened by Sir Frank Price, chairman of the British Waterways Board, 26 November 1980. Disappointingly, the expected rise in freight traffic did not occur. Over the last few years there has been a concentrated effort by the Environment Agency to clean up the Don. In November 2011, the agency announced that they had recently restocked the Don with 1,000 barbel as part of a ten-year programme to help the Don recover from an industrial heritage that had depleted fish stocks.

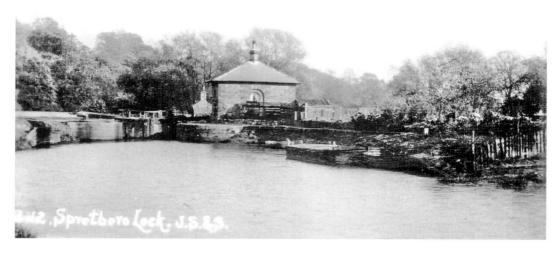

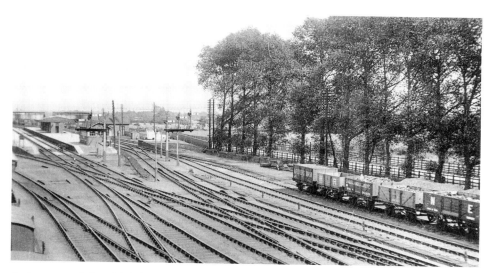

A play on words has titled this view 'A Few Lines from Stainforth'. Facing east, it shows the complex system of railway lines around the station area some of which linked with Hatfield colliery. The Stainforth & Hatfield railway station is on the left. Stainforth railway station was opened by the Manchester Sheffield & Lincolnshire Railway on 1 July 1856. It was replaced on a deviation line on 1 October 1866 and titled Stainforth & Hatfield until 28 September 1992. Thereafter it was known as Hatfield & Stainforth and is currently still open, though the platform buildings have been replaced by simpler structures.

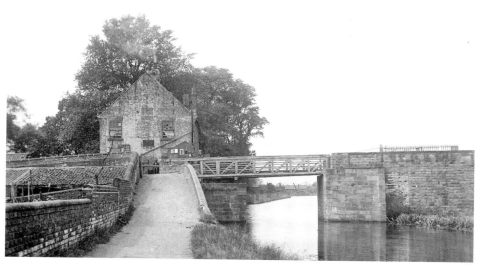

Simonton has taken this shot from the east bank and included the building on the left, formerly occupied by the Black Swan Inn. Barrass (1986) notes premises in existence as the Bridge Inn from at least 1749. Later they were noted as the 'Swan' and the 'Black Swan'. Licensing Registers in the Doncaster MBC Archives Department show the license was not renewed in 1891 but is still shown in the *Doncaster Gazette Directory* of 1893. Thereafter the building existed as a lodging house, surviving until around 1960.

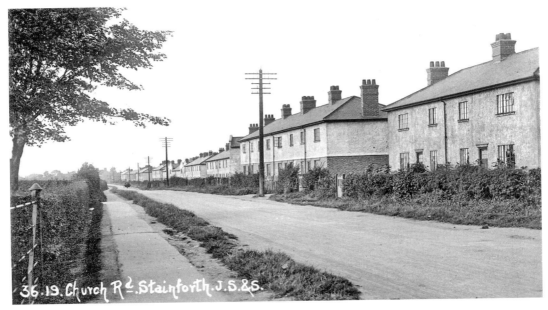

Magilton (1977) stated that much of Stainforth is composed of modern housing catering for the nearby Hatfield colliery, which came into being when the first sod was cut in October 1911. He also adds that until the arrival of the pit, much of Stainforth's prosperity was derived from the Don Navigation, and quite considerable traces survive along the canal bank. Simonton photographed the old and new Stainforth as industrial and new housing developments unfolded, as can be seen in this view facing north of Church Road, stretching between Station Road and the Doncaster Road/Field Road junction.

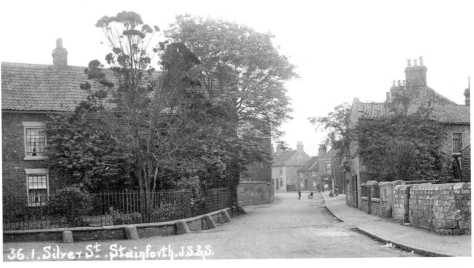

Silver Street links Water Lane and Thorne Road. Kelly (1908) stated that the Hon. Edward Frederick Lindley Wood, of Temple Newsam, Leeds, was the Lord of the Manor and the trustees of the late B. P. Broomhead esq. were the chief landowners, most of the rest of the land being in the hands of small holders.

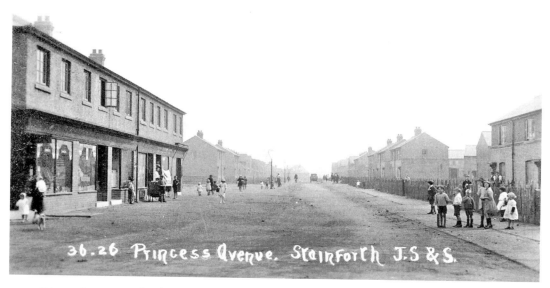

36.26 Princess Avenue. Stainforth J.S & S.

Princess Avenue stretches from Junction Avenue to Field Road. Barrass (1986) relates that no sooner had the first sod for the colliery been cut than sporadic house building began on a small scale on East Lane, later to be followed in the Thorne Road area. As the demand and the scale of building accelerated, with both the council and colliery company playing an active role, it wasn't long before an entirely new village had been created – mainly on the former chapel field. Numerous tales were told of those arriving on the scene to take up employment at the new colliery. Heralded by the engineers and the pit sinkers, as work progressed, their numbers swelled. In many cases the breadwinner arrived alone, living in lodgings until security for the future was established, then sent for the remainder of the family to join them in creating a new life in strange surroundings. The bottom picture shows new commercial premises in Station Road.

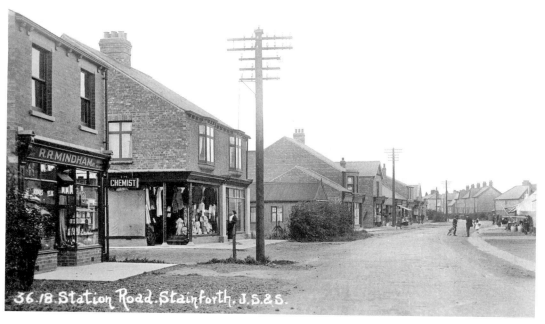

36.18 Station Road. Stainforth. J.S.& S.

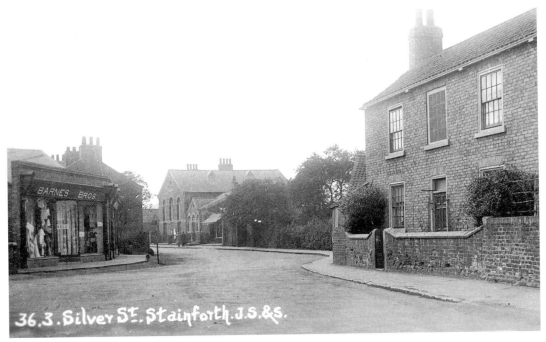

36.3. Silver St. Stainforth. J.S.&S.

Silver Street is seen, with Barnes Bros commercial premises on the left, in the top picture. In the distance is the Primitive Methodist chapel. Noting places of worship in the village, the *Stainforth Official Guide* states that 'the Wesleyan Methodists built a chapel and later a Sunday School in the Fleets in 1820. [A new] Hall and School were opened on 5 November 1925 at a cost of nearly £10,000. The Primitive Methodists have a compact chapel and Sunday School in Silver Street. They date from 1870, previous to which services were held in East Lane, in a building now turned into two dwelling houses. Besides a Roman Catholic Mission Chapel, there is a Gospel Hall in East Lane, and the Salvation Army and the Spiritualist meeting places are in Church Road.' For the bottom picture Simonton is standing in Hall Road facing the Silver Street/Finkle Street junction.

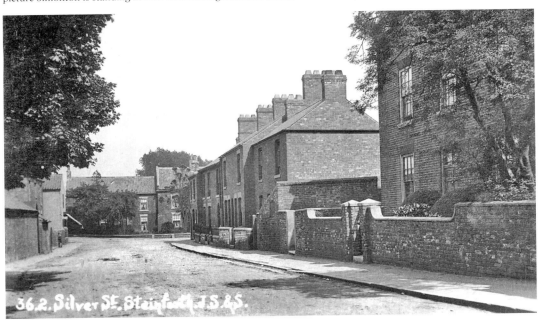

36.2. Silver St. Stainforth. J.S.&S.

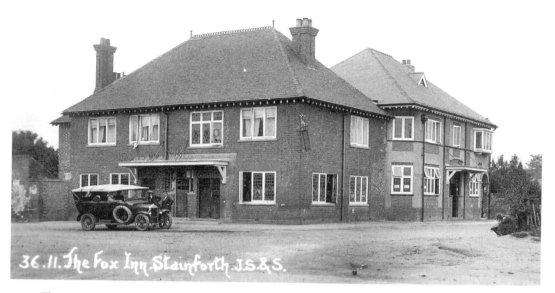

The Fox Inn on Field Road dates from at least 1804. The premises were altered in 1905, 1912, 1922 and 2005. For a brief period in 2005 the pub was retitled 'Goldmine', but has since regained its former name. There were also several other pubs including the King George Hotel, Station Inn, and the New Inn.

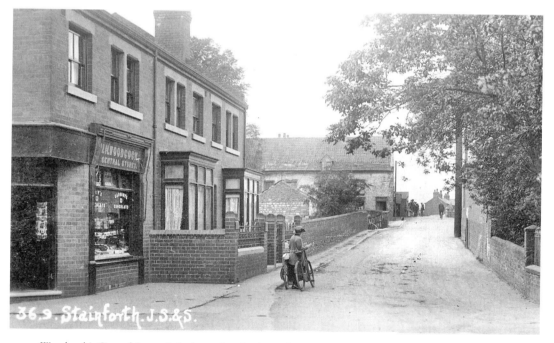

Woodcock's Central Stores, left, situated on Bridge Hill/Water Lane. In 1885, Stainforth became a parish in its own right, breaking away from Hatfield. On 11 September 1925, the *Doncaster Chronicle* reported that 'the Stainforth streets were officially lighted for the first time at 8.30. on Tuesday night, the scheduled lighting up time, by Mr Whitely, the chairman of the Stainforth Parish Council ...'

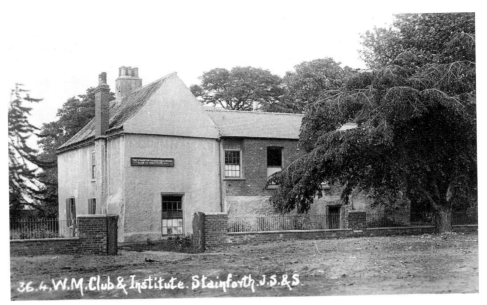

The Stainforth Working Men's Club & Institute. The *Stainforth Official Guide* said the town possessed the British Legion Club, RAOB lodges and various other clubs under good management. It also mentioned that a new Welfare Hall and Institute had opened in December 1928.

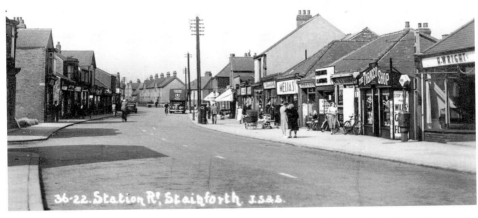

Station Road, stretching between Church Road and the junction with Manor Road and High Street, Hatfield. Traders premises on the right include those belonging to H. Wright; the tobacco shop; Melias, S. & H. Morris; R. C. Hopkinson; Jackson Ltd; and Modern Salons. At one time, half-day closing in Stainforth was on Wednesday. The *Stainforth Official Guide* informed that 'the Post Office is in Station Road, locally called the New Village, and a Sub-post office in Silver Street in the older portion of the Town. Two public call offices are open the same hours as the post offices.'

5

THORNE TO WOODLANDS

THORNE

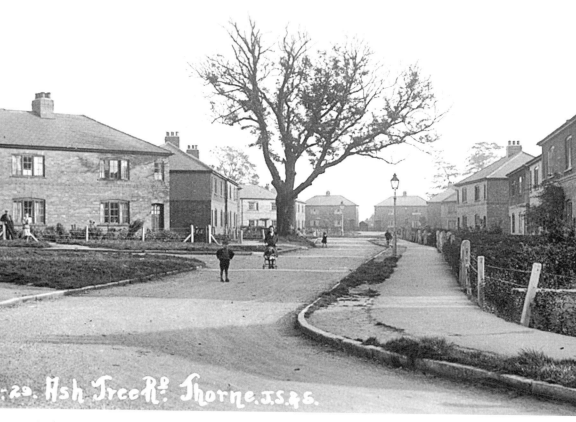

At the time Simonton was an active photographer, Thorne was a small market town, 10 miles north-east from Doncaster and 7 miles south-east from Snaith. Ash Tree Road stretches between Ellison Street and Miller Lane.

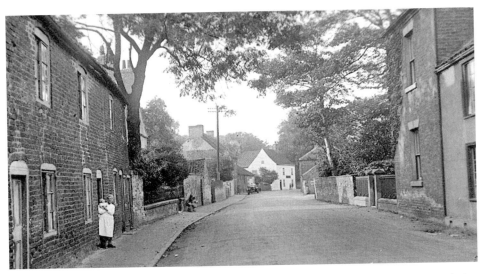

Ellison Street stretches from the South Parade/Bridge Street junction to South End. The view is facing north, with the town centre at the end of the street. Noted properties include Milton House, (right) and Bailey House (off-centre to the left) and Pattricks (large, white painted house), who were blacksmiths, builders and undertakers. Thorne was lighted with gas from works established in 1837 and belonging to a private company. Nos 11, 13, 15, 17, 19, Ellison Street, owned by a Mrs A. E. Wheldon, were cleared under the Thorne No. 19 Clearance Order, 1937.

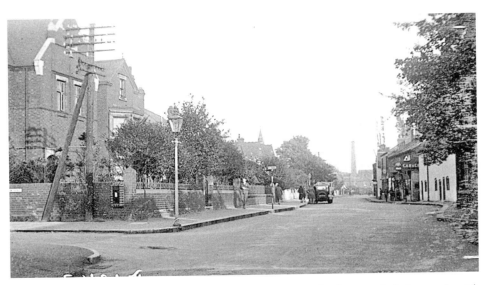

Fieldside links Selby Road to King Street. To take the photograph, Simonton is facing south, with Darley's brewery in the distance. On the left is the Andrew Carnegie Library; the building's foundation stone was laid by James Servant on 14 December 1905. The first lending library in Thorne was established in 1828. Kelly (1908) stated that the library held some 1,600 volumes and was managed by the Parish council. Carnegie was a Scottish philanthropist who set up a trust fund 'for the improvement of mankind'. This included the building of 3,000 public libraries (380 in Britain), the Carnegie Institute of Pittsburgh, the Carnegie Institute of Technology and the Carnegie Institution of Washington for research into the natural and physical sciences.

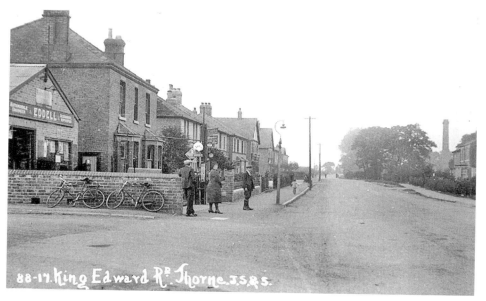

King Edward Road lies between Marshland Road and Field Road. At one time the Hon. Edward Frederick Lindley Wood, of Temple Newsam, Leeds, was Lord of the Manor at Thorne. The principal landowners included the trustees of Makin Durham, James Elmhirst, John Chester Coulman and John Henry Bletcher. Eddell Motors' business premises may be seen on the left.

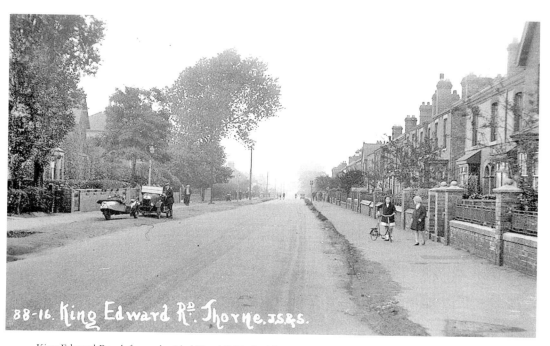

King Edward Road, formerly titled Northfields, looking towards Thorne colliery and Moorends. Besides mining and shipbuilding, Thorne is also noted for its long association with peat cutting, which occurred on the extensive adjacent moorland. Many Thorne people have peat-cutting ancestors, but the activity on Thorne and Hatfield Moors has now ceased and work is being carried out to restore the old workings.

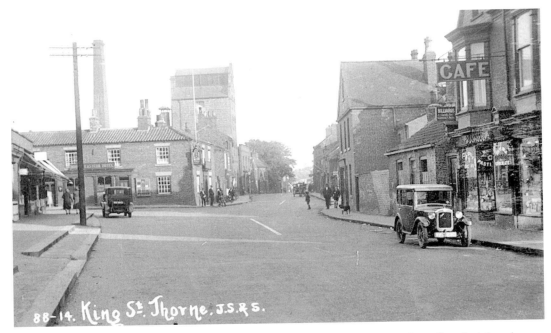

Simonton is looking south from Fieldside towards King Street, with Field Road leading off to the left and Darley's Brewery straight ahead. William Marsdin Darley, born in 1827, was the founder of the Darley Brewing business on the King Street site. The brewery business was taken over by Vaux Breweries of Sunderland in 1978 and closure came eight years later. The brewery tower and façade have been preserved.

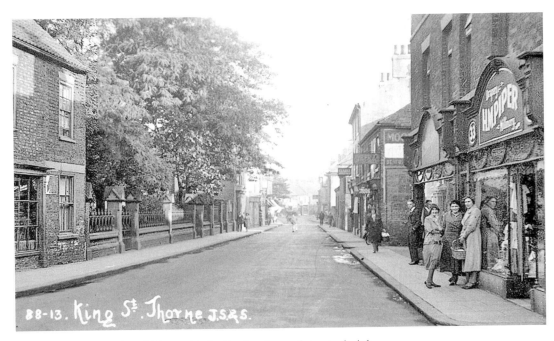

King Street facing south, with Thorne Methodist church out of view to the left.

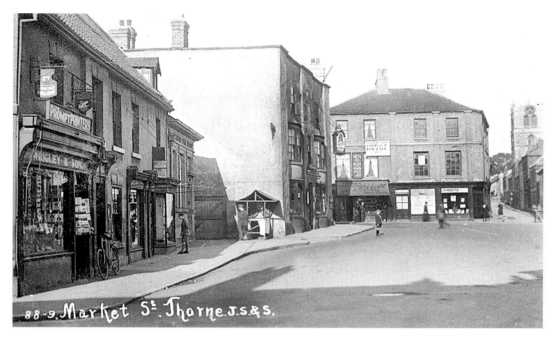

The view is facing east looking along Market Street or Horse Fair Green, towards Church Street on the right and King Street to the left. In 1658 Thorne obtained a Royal Charter to hold markets and it was renewed by King Charles II. The charter also gave Thorne the right to hold two fairs annually. The White Hart Hotel is off-centre to the left, along with the business premises of printer W. Wrigley. The White Hart may be traced to at least 1737. Wrigley's obituary in the *Doncaster Chronicle* 10 April 1931 states that he had lived in Thorne for over fifty years. His business was previously owned by Joseph Mason. The church of St Nicholas is chiefly in the Late Decorated style. It was restored in 1860; the register dating from 1565.

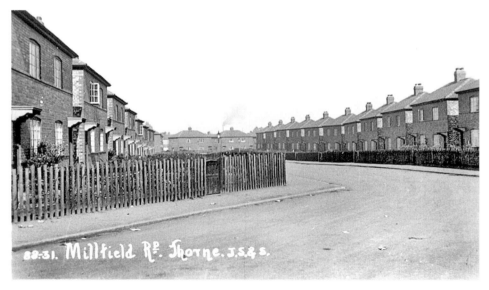

Millfield Road extends from King Edward Road to connect at two points with Lime Tree Grove.

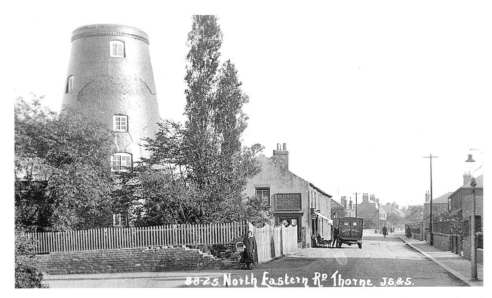

North Eastern Road, following the line of the medieval High Trod, currently extends from King Edward Road. On the left are the business premises of H. Oates, who formerly tenanted the mill. Six other mills are shown in the area on the 1853 Ordnance Survey map ('Z' on the map). During the Second World War, the building was utilised by the Royal Observer Corps to keep watch for enemy aircraft.

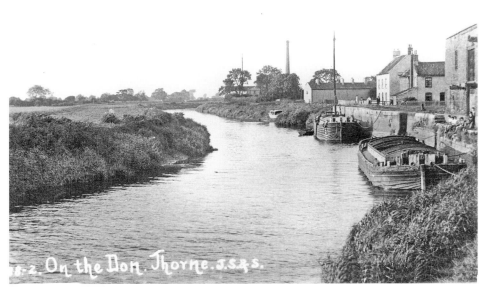

Simonton has found an interesting view here of Thorne Waterside, north-west of the town centre. The area flourished as an inland port during the latter part of the eighteenth and the first part of the nineteenth centuries. It was located at the highest point on the River Don, to which coastal vessels could regularly navigate. Thus, it became an important centre for the transfer of cargoes on to sailing vessels and early steam ships, which made connections between important manufacturing and shipping centres and London. Waterside's trade was diverted to some extent by the emergence of Goole as a port from 1826, but even more traumatic was the introduction of railway services in the area.

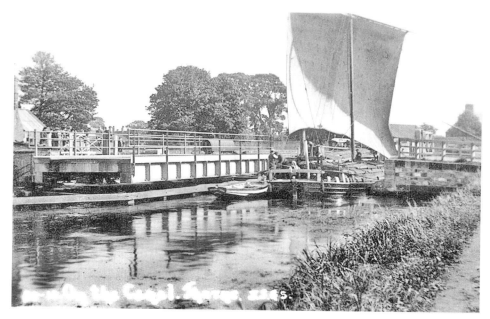

A swing bridge over the canal provides inspiration for Simonton to take a picture here. Nearby was Dunston's shipyard (seen on the left in the picture below) established at Thorne around 1850. Richard Dunston, the founder, transferred his rope-making and ship-rigging business from Torksey, near Lincolnshire. Soon after settling in Thorne he saw the possibilities of barge-building and started the industry for which Thorne became famous. At one time, Dunston's shipyard works covered 3 acres and there were nine berths for barges of up to 300 tons capacity. Numerous types of river and canal trading craft, and at one time eleven steel ships, were turned out yearly. During the Second World War, the firm executed a number of orders for the supply of mine sweepers for the Admiralty. A great deal of repair work was also carried out. Richard Dunston starting by constructing barges of 70–80 tons capacity and later, when his son Thomas went into the business, considerable developments were made. The shipyard once employed approximately 100 men. The area formerly occupied by Dunston's has since been redeveloped for housing.

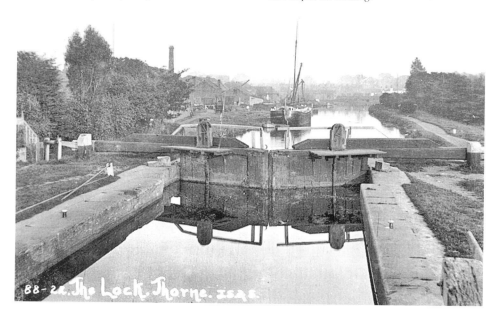

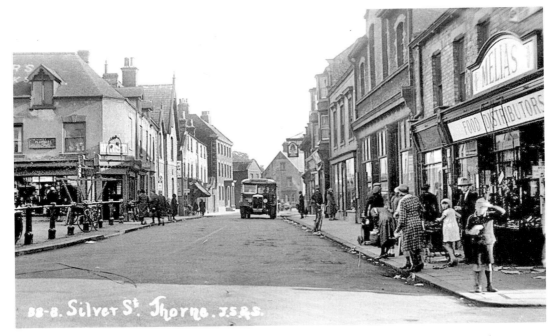

Silver Street extends between the Market Place and South Parade. Simonton has taken this picture facing south. The building on the left, with the pointed gable end, was formerly occupied by William Bunting, a Thorne naturalist, public rights of way campaigner, and often described as 'Thorne Moors Greatest Defender'. The buildings on the right include Melias, food distributors; and further along the sign is visible for the Green Dragon public house, existing from at least 1804 and rebuilt in 1907.

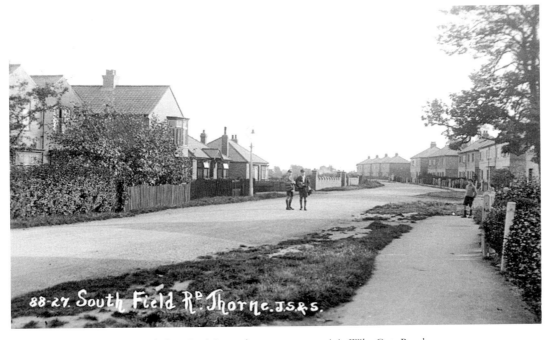

South Field Road stretches south from Back Lane, then curves east to join Wike Gate Road.

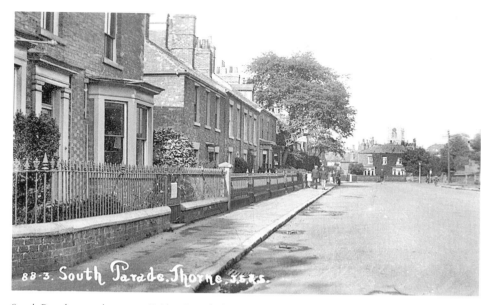

South Parade, once known as Bridge Gate, links Hatfield Road with Silver Street. The photograph has been taken facing east. Out of view to the right is the Memorial Park. Just visible in the distance is the tower of the church of St Nicholas.

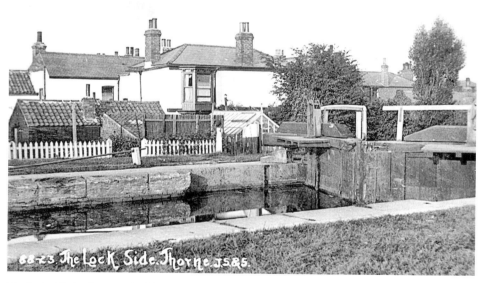

The lock side is photographed here, facing east on the Stainforth & Keadby Canal. During the early twentieth century, the Sheffield Canal, Don Navigation, Stainforth & Keadby Canal and Dearne & Dove Canal merged to become the Sheffield & South Yorkshire Navigation. This formed a direct link between Sheffield and Keadby and the River Trent. At one time the South Yorkshire Railway ran virtually alongside the canal at this point. John Platt, in *Thorne's First Railway*, states that 'the single track line [from Strawberry Island, north of Doncaster, to Thorne] was built by Blyth of Consibrough, and the first train which consisted of ten coal trucks, arrived at Thorne Lock shortly after 12 noon on Tuesday 11 December 1855'.

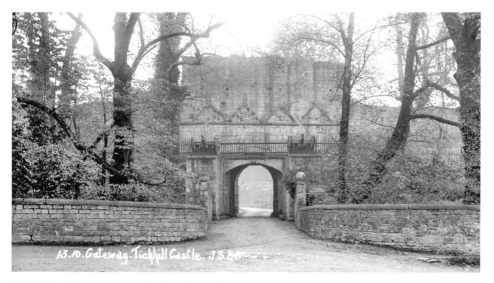

Tickhill Castle gateway possibly dates from the late eleventh century or early twelfth century and is one of the best examples of an early Norman stone-built gatehouse. It probably replaced an earlier wooden structure and is over 10 metres high, with walls over 2 metres thick. In *Tickhill Castle, Yorkshire* it is mentioned that 'Jean de Valois, a French King, was captured during the Battle of Poitiers in 1356 and brought to England by the Black Prince, son of Edward III. It is believed he was kept in Tickhill gatehouse as a prisoner.'

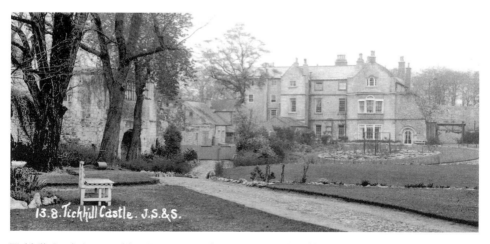

Tickhill Castle is owned by Her Majesty the Queen, in right of her Duchy of Lancaster. Following the Civil War, the existing castle keep and domestic buildings were demolished. John Leyland visited 'Tickhil', noting that 'all the buildings withyn the (Castle) area be down, saving an old haulle'. The Hall may have stood against the wall just south of the gatehouse. A roof-mark of the gable end can be seen on the bailey wall. The house seen here was probably built by the Hansby family towards the end of the sixteenth or in the early seventeenth century. In *Tickhill Castle, Yorkshire* it is stated that 'the house has basically had three stages of development but retains a lot of its seventeenth-century character. The house was last occupied in 1978.'

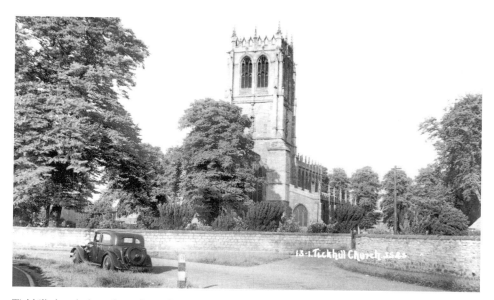

Tickhill church dates from the early 1100s and is predominantly of Perpendicular style, with glimpses of earlier Norman (semi-circular headed doorway leading to the tower stairs), Early English (lancet windows) and Decorated (two fine windows) traits. It was built from magnesian limestone quarried from the valley close to Roche Abbey and is a Grade I listed building. The church consists of nave with aisles and clerestory; chancel with side chapels; north and south porches and a lofty square tower. The west end opens to the nave and aisles by three elegant arches. The register dates from 1542 and in 1859 the church was first lit with gas.

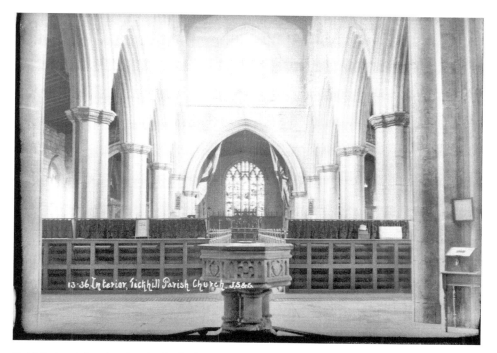

Tickhill church interior, showing in the distance the choir stalls and altar.

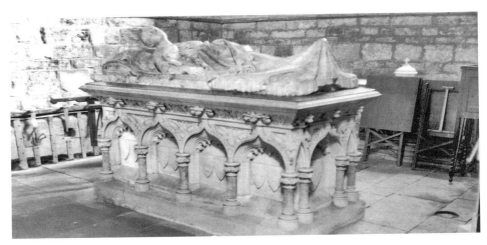

The Foljambe memorial, by William Calder Marshall, depicts Louisa Blanche Foljambe (*née* Howard) with her baby son resting on a tomb, and is located in the north-west corner of the church. Louisa died in childbirth in 1871. On www.tickhillhistorysociety.org.uk it is related that 'such was Cecil's grief at the loss of his wife, six weeks after their day-old second son Frederick died, that he commemorated Louisa in a total of at least sixty-two memorials in thirty-eight churches'. Decorating the sides of the tomb are heraldic shields relating to both Louisa's and her husband George's ancestry. George Savile Foljambe became Earl of Liverpool in 1905. Calder Marshall was the most prolific exhibitor of statuary at the Royal Academy in the Victorian age.

WADWORTH

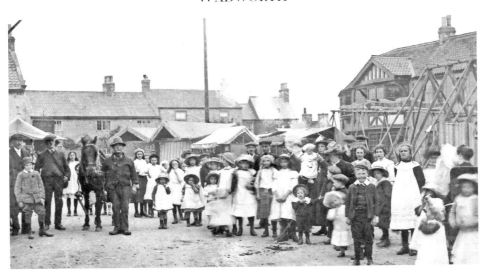

With this view Simonton has tried to capture the atmosphere of the Wadworth Maypole festivities. The people are gathered along Main Street facing south-east, with the White Hart public house to the right and the Fox Inn just out of view on the left. The *Doncaster Gazette* of 6 June 1935 said that the Wadworth Maypole Festival is essentially a day for the village children – a day which the little ones look forward to with keen anticipation. 'The custom has been carried on almost unbroken for many centuries and was made possible year by year through the work of the Maypole Committee and others.' Maypole festivities are still carried out today in Wadworth.

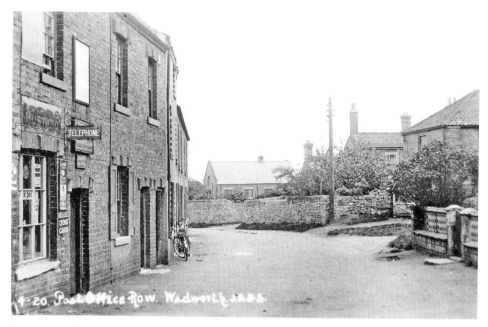

Two views of Post Office Row on Low Street (also known as Carr Lane), which extended in a south-easterly direction from Main Street to Well Lane (known locally as Low Road). A Wesleyan chapel is located in the centre. All the properties on the thoroughfare, Nos 1–44, were cleared under the Wadworth (Nos 1, 2, and 3) Compulsory Purchase Orders of 1963. Prior to this, it was argued at a public enquiry that the Rural District Council were trying to make the CPO an excuse for taking more land than they really needed to rehouse the tenants of the village. Only fifty-three new units were required, but the council was proposing to create ninety-nine, because, it was alleged, they were intending to house people from Loversall. For the council, E. O. Thompson said that most of the houses concerned were unfit for human habitation.

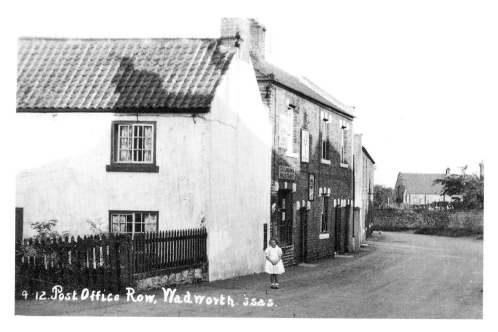

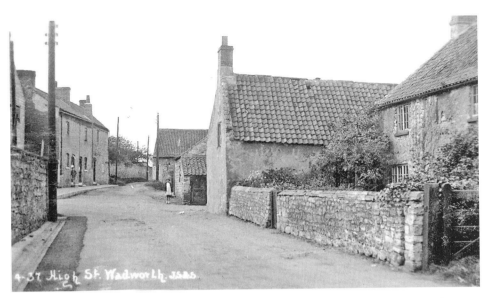

High Street extends north-west from Main Street. This view is looking towards Welbeck Close, out of view to the right. A number of the properties no longer exist, being cleared in the 1963 Wadworth Clearance Orders. At one time F. J. S. Foljambe was Wadworth's Lord of the Manor. On www. doncasterfhs.co.uk it is mentioned that 'by the fifteenth century a branch of the Fitzwilliam family of Sprotbrough had settled in Wadworth, as witnessed by two fine tombs of that period still to be found in the church. This branch moved its seat to Aldwark, some 7 miles east along the River Don, on inheriting the estate through marriage. Both Aldwark and Wadworth passed by similar means to the Foljanbe family.' The church register dates from 1575.

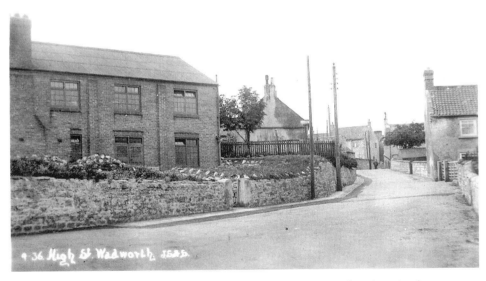

High Street from a standpoint further south than the previous picture. Magilton (1977) makes some very erudite comments about Wadworth: 'A village chiefly of stone-built small houses, cottages and farms, partly ruined by modern housing development and wholesale demolition … If this has served any useful purpose, it is perhaps a warning to the district to preserve what remains of similar villages in the area.'

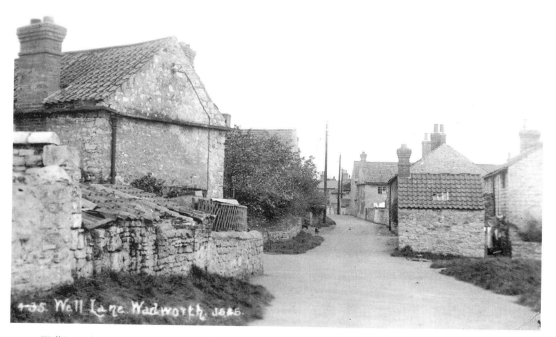

Well Lane, known locally as Low Road, stretched south-east from Sweet Lane to link with Low Street (Carr Lane). A number of properties were demolished along here as a result of the Wadworth CPO of 1963.

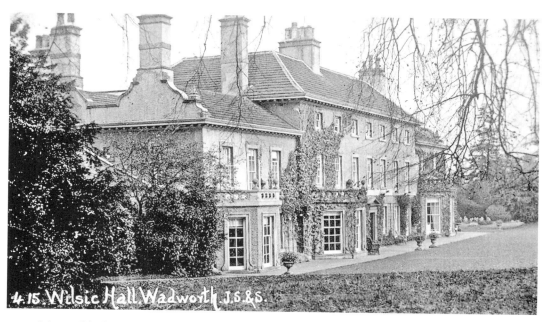

It is possible that Wilsic Hall, situated south of Wadworth, occupies the site of a smaller Tudor house and was built between 1720 and 1740 for Sir Francis Tofield. Among the previous owners are the Barnsley Co-operative Society and Lt Griffith. In later years Wilsic Hall was a country club, but it is presently occupied by the Hesley Group of Schools. The Hall received a Grade II listing in June 1968, and English Heritage state that the building has nineteenth-century additions and alterations.

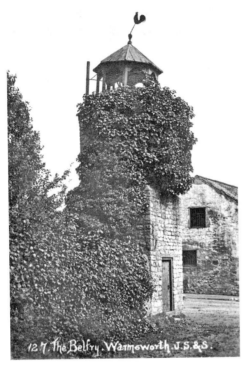

127. The Belfry. Warmsworth. J.S.&S.

Magilton and Hey (1983) state that the Warmsworth parish church, 1 kilometre from the village centre, 'is unusually sited, and until the completion of the present church, services were announced in the village by a bell attached to a tower [seen here] of unknown date at the end of the parsonage croft near the gates of [the east side of] Warmsworth Hall'. The two authors argue that although no specific reason can be given for the separation of the church and village, the 'complex manorial history of the parish provides contexts in which a shift in settlement could have occurred'.

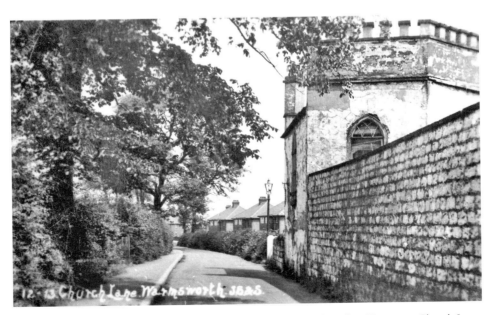

12-13. Church Lane Warmsworth J.S.&S.

A curious Bothy, a summer house in the corner of the garden of the White House, on Church Lane, has caught the attention of Simonton here. Unfortunately, the building was swept away during the construction of the A1 motorway and Church Lane no longer exists in this section.

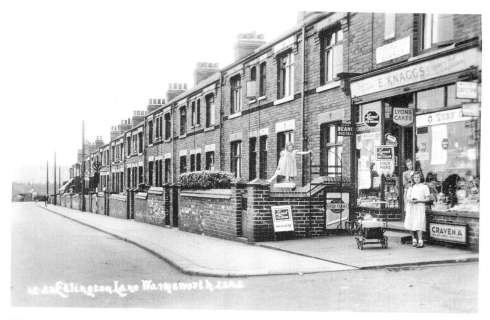

The *Doncaster Gazette* of 10 June 1910 ran an article headed 'Projected Building at Warmsworth' and stated that between two and three hundred houses were expected to be built in the area within 'the next year or two ... for the accommodation of a big influx of population ... this new population ... will be of the mining class in the main'. The site of the projected new houses was on the estate of Lady Isabella Battie-Wrightson (of Cusworth Hall) adjacent to the crossroads. This stretch of housing on the western side of Edlington Lane looking south was part of the building project and features Knagg's corner shop.

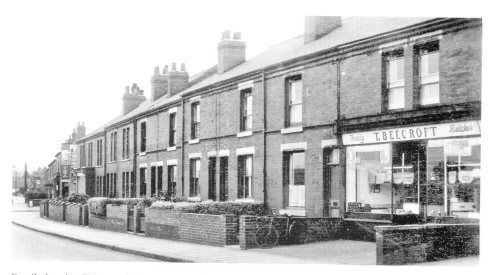

Family butcher T. Beecroft's business premises, on the west side of Edlington Lane, were photographed by Simonton looking towards Edlington. In an earlier view of the same location Simonton shows that the premises were occupied by W. Brown's general stores. With the existence of the large Co-operative Society stores further along the road, with various provision departments, opened in 1913, trade at one time must have been quite buoyant as nothing similar exists today. All the properties survive, but Brown's/Beecroft's old shop is currently a unisex hair salon. The entrance to Wrightson Avenue is seen on the left.

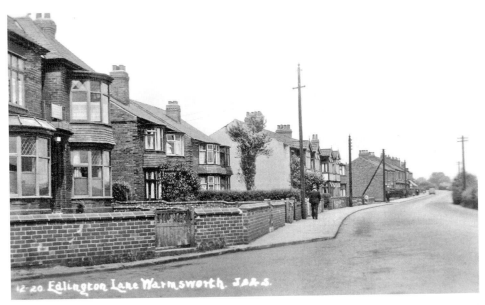

The *Doncaster Gazette* of 8 October 1920 stated that the Doncaster Rural District Council had instructed their surveyor to number and name the streets of Warmsworth. Edlington Lane facing north has been photographed here. On the left is the Graceholme Social Working Men's Club & Institute, formed in 1936. News of the club's opening was reported in the *Doncaster Chronicle* of 10 September 1936; J. Jones, a member of Warmsworth Parish Council, was elected as president. Out of view to the left was the Hull & Barnsley Railway Co.'s goods station. In the distance on the left is the entrance to Cecil Avenue.

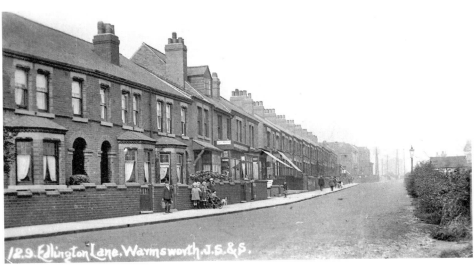

Several more shops are evident here on Edlington Lane, facing north, and none are existing today, being converted to private dwellings. In the distance are the Co-operative Society's stores and Simonton has used his powers of persuasion to encourage a number of children to pose for him. Under the heading of 'Edlington Lane Footpath', the *Doncaster Gazette* of 3 March 1922 reported that a start had begun with the making of Edlington Lane footpath. The Warmsworth Parish Council clerk stated that the Rural Council had been recommended to accept a tender of £416 for the work.

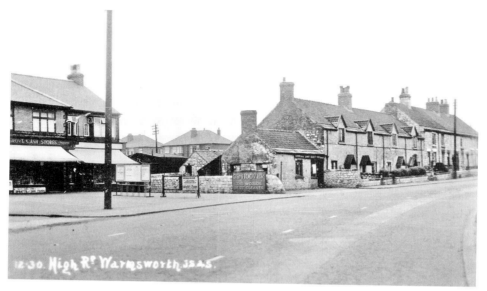

Simonton has photographed the north side of High Road here and included the Beech Grove stores on the left. For a number of years the store was occupied by the Ogden family, and later by Ron and Val Craven. Advertising hoardings on the forecourt give details of the films being shown at the Windsor Cinema in Balby and mention *Indian Uprising* and *Desert Legion*. The single-storey stone property in the centre, formerly a smithy's, was later occupied by shoe repairer Fred Lowrey and after him, Trevor Miller, with an electrical repair centre. All the properties still survive today, although in an altered state.

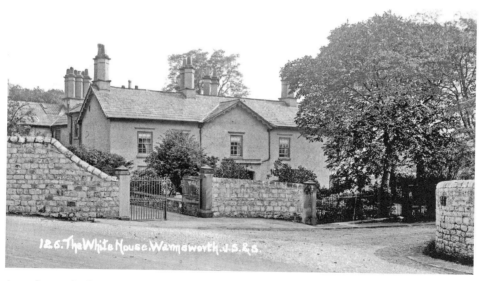

According to the *Doncaster Gazette*, 11 December 1958, the White House 'is estimated to be at least 300 years old. The building, a fine example of Georgian architecture, was built by the Aldam family, whose ancestral home had been at Warmsworth since before the Conquest. In fact the building is still owned by the Warde-Aldam family, of Frickley Hall.' The house's tenants at this time were Mr and Mrs G. M. Frampton, and Mrs Ethel Briggs; each renting part of the house as their homes. Both had to move out when the White House was demolished around 1960 as part of the A1 motorway scheme.

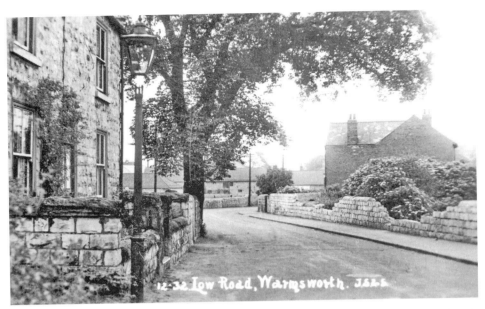

12-32 Low Road, Warmsworth. 3525

At one time a section of the Doncaster to Sheffield main road ran along Low Road West (seen here in both pictures), past Warmsworth Hall and through Low Road East. Magilton and Hey (1983) state that quarries lying in the north-western corner of the parish, where the Don runs in a deep gorge through the limestone, may have been exploited during the Roman period, and supplied the principal building material for Warmsworth into modern times. Magilton (1977) wrote that Warmsworth is a typical limestone village centred around Warmsworth Hall, and that 'redevelopment in the village centre until recently has been minimal and its character has consequently been maintained'. But in subsequent years, along both Low Road West and Low Road East there has been much infilling with new properties and the redevelopment of existing ones. Unfortunately this has not always been in keeping with the character of the area.

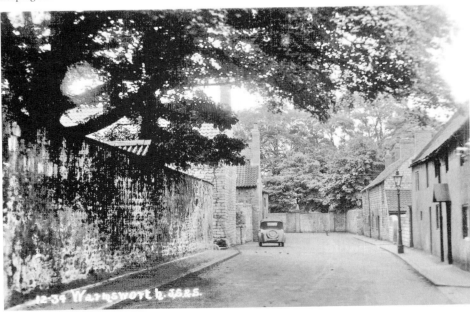

12-34 Warmsworth. 3525

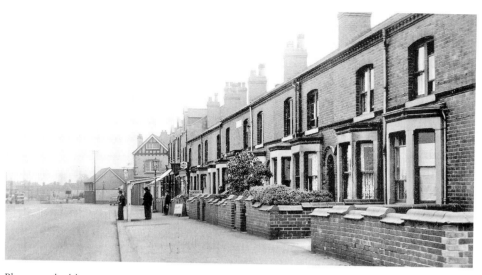

Photographed here are properties on Sheffield Road's southern side, looking to the junction with High Road and Edlington Lane. In the distance is a gable of the Cecil & Battie-Wrightson Arms. The *Doncaster Gazette* of 20 April 1923 reported that there was a debate over whether the road from the Co-operative Stores towards Conisbrough was Sheffield Road or High Road. Warmsworth Parish Council decided to adhere to the name 'Sheffield Road'. One of the properties on the right contains the post office. In later years it was run by the Lumb family and then by the Sadlers, but it closed in 2012.

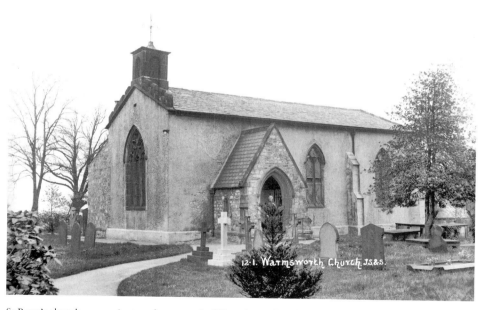

St Peter's church was a nineteenth-century building situated to the north-east of Warmsworth village. It was replaced in 1942 by a church on a new site nearer the village. The old church was later demolished due to vandalism. In November 1977 an archaeological dig was commenced on the site to discover the extant of the church's medieval predecessors, thought from documentary sources to date to around 1170 or earlier. Results of the excavation and details of two other churches on the site are recorded in 'St Peter's Church, Warmsworth', published in the *Yorkshire Archaeological Journal*, Vol. 55.

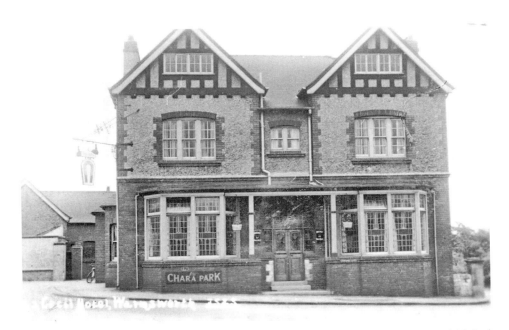

A new hotel for Warmsworth opened on 13 February 1911, replacing the Barrell Inn, which had existed on Low Road East from at least 1822. The Cecil & Battie Wrightson Arms, situated at the High Road/Edlington Lane junction, was built by local builder Wortley. The pub was sold by R. C. Battie-Wrightson to John Smith's Brewery in 1931 and the name shortened to Cecil in 1959. The premises were demolished in 1959, and a new pub erected on a site set back from the road junction. The Cecil closed in 2008 and is currently an Indian restaurant.

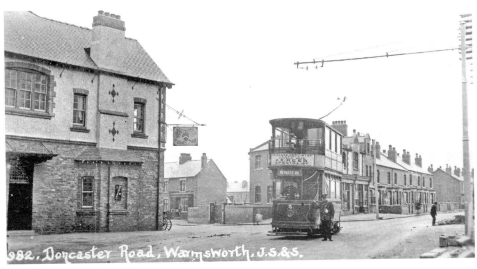

The Balby tram route was extended to Warmsworth in 1915, and initially the outer terminus was situated outside the Cecil & Battie Wrightson Arms public house, seen on the left. But in 1919 a short spur was laid along Edlington Lane, to the left, after which time the trams stopped adjacent to the Co-operative Society's building. The tram is working on a cross-town service to Beckett Road, in operation between 1915 and 1917. Trams operated for the last time on the Balby/Warmsworth route on 25 July 1931. Thereafter, Balby was served by trolleybuses, while Warmsworth was served by motor buses travelling to Edlington.

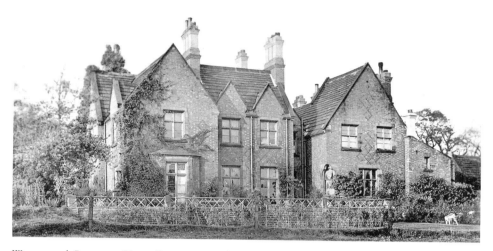

Warmsworth Parsonage House/Rectory was enlarged and altered by the Revd Charles Edward Thomas around 1861. He was one of the most noted Warmsworth rectors, and held the position for nearly thirty years. Alterations and improvements were made to the building throughout the twentieth century, before it was converted to flats in the 1970s and subsequently demolished. A new, smaller rectory was eventually built on an adjacent site.

WOODLANDS

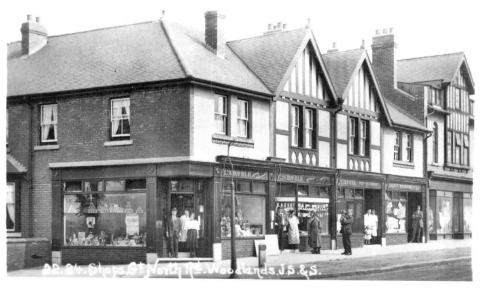

The first sod was cut for Brodsworth colliery on 23 October 1905. The pit was sunk jointly by the Staveley Coal & Iron Co. and the Hickleton Main Colliery Co. The man behind the operation was Arthur Markham, who not only planned a large colliery but was also determined to house the men and their families under the best possible conditions. Consequently, Woodlands is an example of a private village built expressly to house the people working for a colliery company. Woodlands' model village was designed by Chesterfield architect Percy B. Houfton during 1907–8. A view of the shops on the Great North Road, skirting the model village, is seen here.

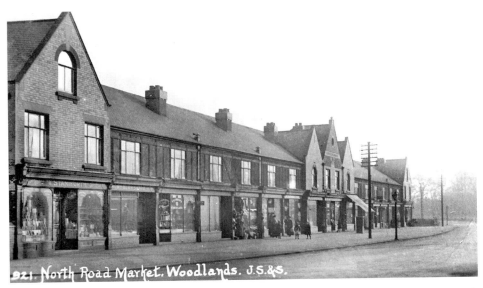

Architect Percy Houfton was influenced by the industrial community ideals of the late nineteenth century and the emerging Garden City Movement, and Woodlands became an early and influential town-planning scheme. Though the private property of the colliery company, it was intended that the village should pay, and at the rent charged it was expected to bring in a return of 4 per cent on the capital after everything including ground rent, rates and maintenance was paid. This picture is one of several taken by Simonton of the shops on the Great North Road.

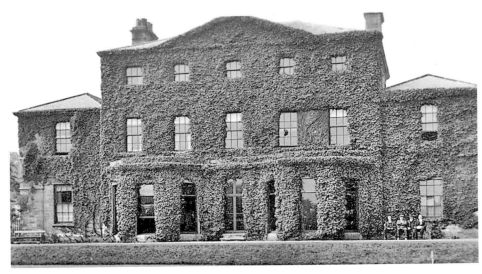

Brodsworth Institute, formerly titled the Woodlands, or Woodlands Hall, was built by Thomas Bradford. An 1819 sale notice described the property as a substantial, elegant mansion, presenting a handsome and uniform elevation, replete with stabling for eight horses. Gordon Smith in the *Doncaster Gazette*, 13 January 1966, records that 'although the architecture of the house, is not in the highest classical taste, it is well proportioned, being built of red brick the centre block being headed by a three-bay pediment'. Thomas Walker was one of the Hall's noted occupants and before he died in 1891, aged eighty-two, was one of the oldest magistrates of the West Riding. During the twentieth century, the Woodlands became the Park Club.

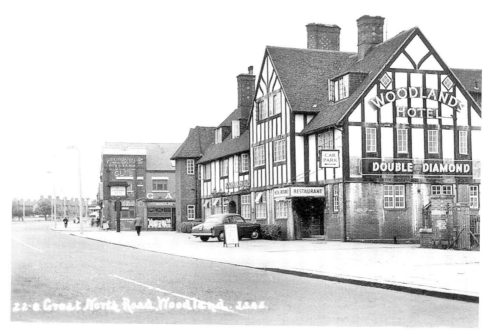

The model village was built in two phases and included primary and secondary schools, a Methodist chapel and Church of England place of worship, a health centre and church hall. The community buildings were centrally situated between the two phases to provide better education and a deeper sense of spiritual values. The *Doncaster Chronicle* of 14 March 1913, under the heading 'Erection of Shops and Houses', noted the development of the area on the opposite side of the Great North Road – east of the model village. Later, a cinema and a public house were erected within the row of shops. The public house was built in 1914 by the People's Refreshment House Association Ltd. The hotel is clearly visible in the top picture with the side elevation of the cinema off-centre to the left. Another view of the parade of shops is seen in the picture below.

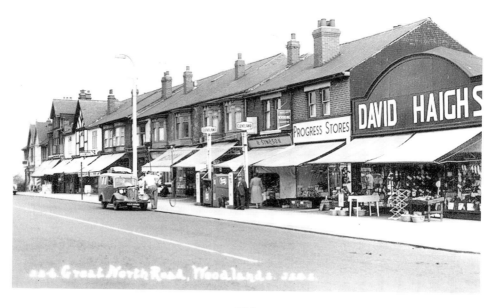

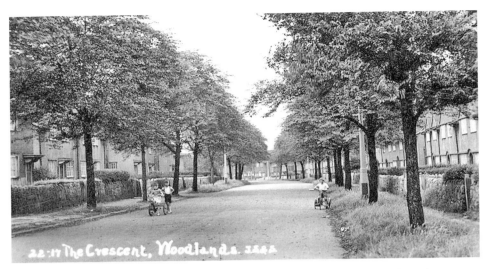

The first part of the model village to be developed – known as the Park - contained 121 houses, at a density of five to the acre, overlooking a 24-acre green, surrounded by well-established trees. To retain as much as possible of the original site's character, a single-track road was taken around the open grass following the line of the shrubbery, and the cottages were built in a quadrangle to face on to the open space. Woodlands is also significant in respect of the design and internal layout of its houses. There are nineteen different styles of architecture represented, in order to avoid the monotony and uniformity of terraced housing. The Crescent, depicted here, almost encircles the model village.

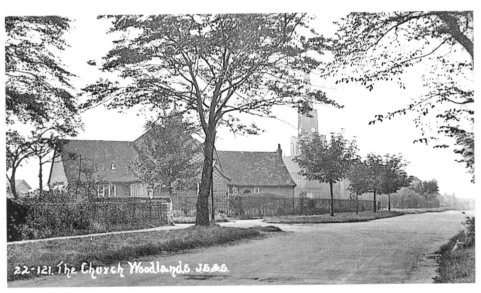

'At the beginning of the twentieth century Methodism made a vigorous and successful bid to mission the coalmining villages that sprang up around Doncaster. In 1913 a committee was established with representatives from the Wesleyan Methodists and Primitive Methodists to discuss "preventing overlapping and arranging for better distribution of service" in the Yorkshire Coalfield,' wrote Geoffrey Morris in *The Story of Methodism in Doncaster and District 1743– 1988*. The Methodist chapel at Woodlands is pictured here.

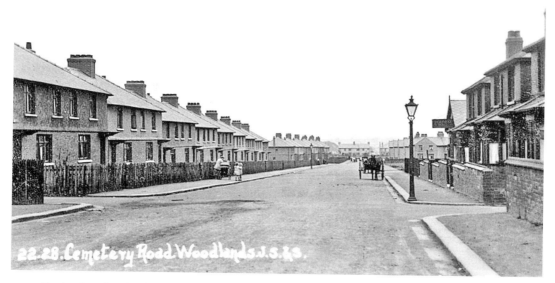

22-28 Cemetery Road Woodlands J.S.&J.

Further housing developments at Woodlands were undertaken on the east side of the Great North Road by Adwick Urban District Council around 1920. The project consisted of approximately 272 houses, and they were built in pairs and made up the thoroughfares that included Princess Street, Windmill Balk Lane, Cemetery Road, and Villa Road. The top picture shows Cemetery Road, extending from the Great North Road and giving access to Villa Road. Princess Street, linking the Great North Road and Doncaster Lane, is shown below.

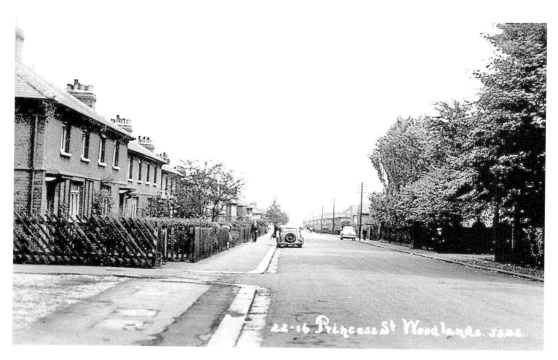

22-16 Princess St Woodlands. J.S.&J.

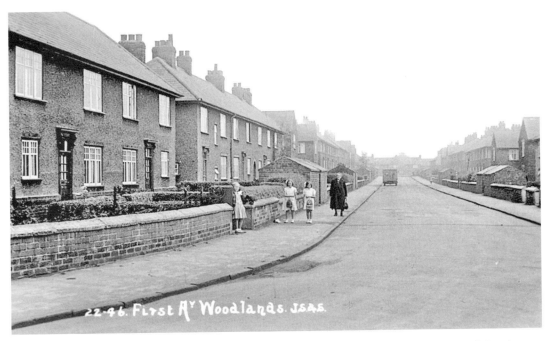

22-46. First Av. Woodlands. JS45.

Adwick Council built a further 294 houses – in identical pairs – on the east side of the Great North Road from 1927, and amongst the streets were Grosvenor Road, Caxton Road and Stafford Road. Brodsworth Main Colliery Co. joined the Industrial Housing Association during the early 1920s and under this scheme approximately 552 more houses were built during the mid-1920s between the Great North Road and Doncaster Lane. These houses formed the streets of First Avenue, Second Avenue, Third Avenue, Fourth Avenue, Fifth Avenue, Lake Road, Welfare Road and Tudor Road. First Avenue, extending from Welfare Road to Grange Road, is seen in the top picture and Third Avenue, extending from Welfare Road, in the one below.

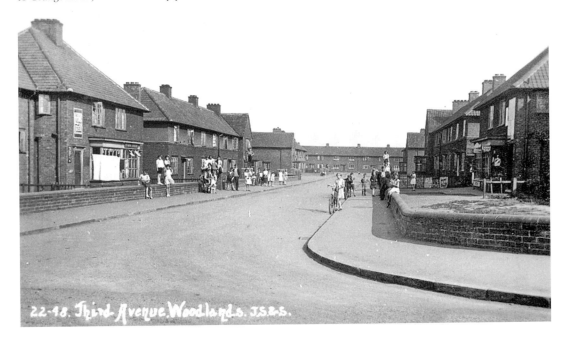

22-48. Third Avenue. Woodlands. JS25.

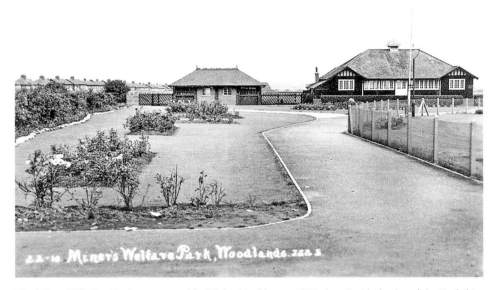

The Miners' Welfare Park was opened by Violet Markham and Herbert Smith, leader of the Yorkshire Miners' Association, on Saturday 25 July 1925. The Miners' Welfare Institute and 12 acres of land had cost around £11,200. Further extensions were added in the late 1920s.

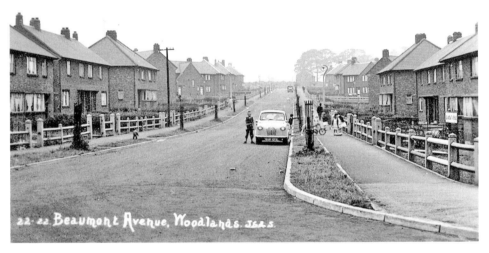

Post-war housing developments in Woodlands included another estate on the north side of Ridge Balk Lane. The layout reflected that of the original model village, and Beaumont Avenue, seen here linking the Circuit and Elmwood Avenue, was one of a number of streets in the area. The ownership of the Woodlands colliery estates was passed to the NCB when the coal industry was nationalised, and then to the Doncaster Metropolitan Council around 1981. The quality of the original estate was recognised by the Doncaster MBC back in 1978, when it was declared a Conservation Area. Ten years later, the Department of the Environment announced that sixty houses out of 653, along with four principal community buildings, warranted listed building status, as they were of national importance. The listed cottages were the ones which had survived extensive alterations.

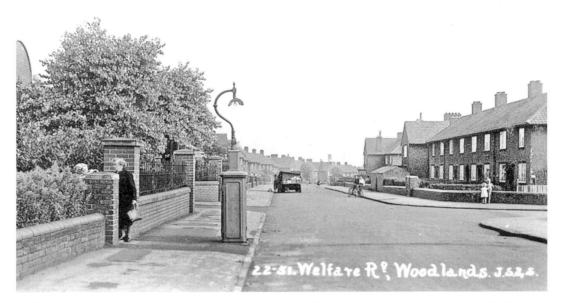

Welfare Road links the Great North Road with Doncaster Lane; Simonton is quite happy to capture two ladies chatting in this view.

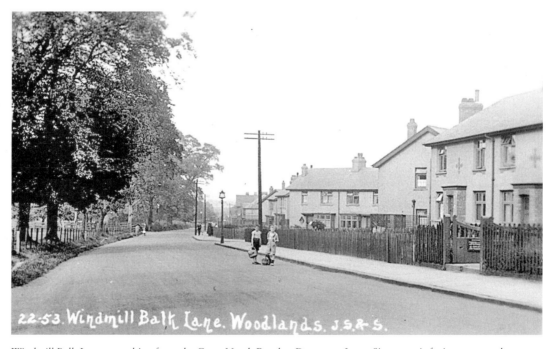

Windmill Balk Lane, stretching from the Great North Road to Doncaster Lane; Simonton is facing east to take this photograph.